EMOTIONAL

PRISONS

Ken Gross

EMOTIONAL

PRISONS

BOOK ONE

ORIGINS

Table of Contents

Acknowledgements

My most important acknowledgement must be to my parents, **Cyril and Barbara Gross**. They faced the impossible choice of abandoning me to save my life. In 1956, at three years old, I was diagnosed with Tuberculosis, which was most likely a death sentence back then in England. They faced the choice of putting me into a long-term sanatorium with the hope of healing, or keeping me living with them in London, a city that had a daily smog warning. They chose hope: how could I not acknowledge them!

Next, I'd like to acknowledge my wife, **Danita**. She is the one who has loved me and put up with my acting out: the 'crazy making' and the insecurity of living with an emotionally trapped person for so many years.

I must recognize my personal counselor, **Tim Mavergeorge**, who helped me to connect all the dots in my life and finally come to understand myself.

There have been pastors who had a part making unseen contributions to my soul, by influencing my thinking and they have added to this book in some way. **Tim Sledge, John Crawford, Alex Kennedy, Mike McGown and Jerry Edmonson.**

My men's prayer group, a place of refuge and safety for 19 years has been a constant source of acceptance, encouragement and strength.

I would also like to thank those that have helped with the editing process. Particularly **Kelly Wagler,** a fellow traveler in the difficult journey of life and **Kathy Trout**, my final editor, whose wonderful perfectionistic tendencies were very helpful at the end of the production of this book.

About the Author

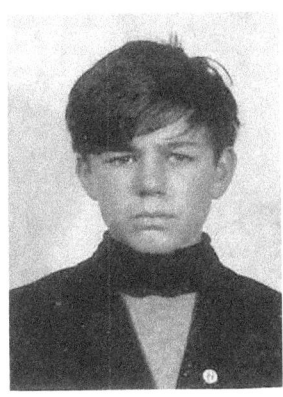

The author: age fourteen

Perhaps you note the serious demeanor.

Yes, my troubles started early. An intense child destined to struggle in life at 14. I was in my first emotional prison at age 15: the prison of false intimacy. I struggled with security, performance issues, acceptance and irresponsibility all my life.

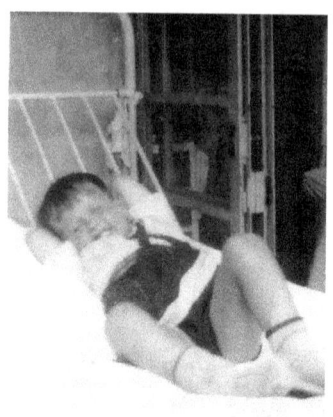

I was an abandoned child at three.

In this picture, I am seemingly so happy go lucky, yet I was living in a sanatorium with Tuberculosis In the picture, I had a white strap across me used to tie me down in bed at night, because I would get up and wake up the rest of the very sick children.

Finally, Christ got hold of me when I was ready and revealed me to myself; He told me of my troubles and explained how to be healed. The pages of this book, and the two that follow, expose some of my life as they share the story of emotional prisons. *Ken Gross*

This is me now.

I was born in England in 1953 on an RAF base. My dad was 20 and mum 17. They had six more boys, but no girls, over the next few years; the last boy passed away within 24 hours of his birth. He was the brother I never met.

I contracted tuberculosis at three, was placed into long term care, and released 21 months later. I attended schools in my home town of Welwyn Garden City, about 20 miles north of London. I went to an elite high school (called a grammar school in the UK), attended the University of London through an outreach program, from which I obtained an undergraduate degree in Physics and Chemistry. A few years later I attended the University of Oklahoma, also through outreach, and received an MBA. I have been working in the financial services industry in the Houston area since 1986.

I currently reside in Katy, Texas with my wife and two dogs. I attend a local church, and run a ministry called Merimnao, which is mentioned on the next page.

Ministry

In 2009 I had a vision for ministry; a ministry for those trapped in emotional prisons, a ministry for those who were brokenhearted. In 2010 it was put into action. Thus was born "Merimnao" which is a Greek word that is often translated as burdens, anxieties, troubles or cares.

Go to www.merimnao.org to find out more about how we are helping others get out of their emotional prisons, overcome their compulsions and addictions, and move toward healing.

As the director of the ministry, I get to put a lot of the ideas laid out in the three "Emotional Prisons" books into practice. It is a fulfilling work, and I am blessed by God by being allowed to help Him as He heals people through it.

Ken Gross

Prologue

I don't really have much to say in introducing this series of three books.

The whole idea of being trapped by emotions was birthed out of dealing with the dysfunctional behaviors in my own life. I actually wrote this book four years ago in 2008 and 2009, and I got sidetracked by ministry, but it is time to publish my ideas.

The three books are simply constructed:

Book 1 – Emotional Prisons – Origins

I deal with what an emotional prison is and explain where they come from or how they are formed. I also give the reader a method of analyzing them, identifying the four major root emotional issues they stimulate the formation of them in a person's life.

Book 2 – Emotional Prisons - Prisons

In this book I go into detail about some of the major emotional prisons that exist. Three of the chapters are about religious emotional prisons, including a candid look at the Christian version.

Book 3 – Emotional Prisons - Healing

In this book we get a look at the following things:

1. Ten Principles of Healing.
2. Twelve Barriers to Healing.
3. Seven Healing Choices.

Then I finish this last book with a chapter on conclusions I have drawn from writing the series.

EMOTIONAL PRISONS

PART 1

THE SOUL

The Soul, the inner part of a human, is somewhat of a mystery to most people. If a person does not understand the Soul then they cannot understand why some people are evil, why some seem to be good and gracious and why some seem to get trapped in their compulsions or addictions.

In the first section of this book, we are going to take a look at how the Soul works as a foundation for understanding the nature of an emotional prison. More importantly, we are going to get a glimpse of where a person can go to find the key to opening up the spiritual jail that they are in.

ORIGINS

You don't have a Soul. You are a Soul. You have a body.
C. S. Lewis

Do you feel trapped, stifled or smothered? Are you rattled sometimes by your own behavior? Do you treat people around you badly? Are you feeling like doing something you know violates your values? Are you a control freak? If you answered, "YES" to any of these questions then you may be locked away in your own personal "Emotional Prison."

Consider John, a real person from my past, but not his actual name. John was charming, he was good looking, and he was lonely even though he had a good-looking wife and two adorable kids. Then this man found his way into a role with his company where he would interact directly with the public on company product issues. Over a period of time John developed close relationships with some of the female customers who just loved his personal attention. It wasn't long before John was having an affair, followed by another, and another. His co-workers, including myself, knew, but did nothing about it. John was firmly in jail, an emotional jail, and he had put himself there.

What about Alice, a sister of a friend? She was the life of the party from her early teenage years, a good, clean and decent girl. Her parents helped and encouraged her all the way, giving her everything she needed to remain popular in high school. College changed it all. Alice discovered beer, and it seemed to her that her new friends liked her even more than her old friends. Then with the beer came the cigarettes, and the wine, and pot smoking, and I'm sure you guessed it, hard drugs. Alice too, had become stuck in her own personal prison cell, locked in by her emotional needs.

I could repeat numerous stories like this, and I'm sure that we all have people in our lives that have either put themselves in an emotional prison, or been forced into one by circumstances.

In these books, I will identify the type of emotional prison that John and Alice have put themselves into, together with several others. First though we ought to explore the question:

- **What is an emotional prison?**

I want to answer this by first saying that I really like simple explanations, reasons for things that I can get my mind around without being a rocket scientist. That is what I'm going to attempt to do here.

Contemplate for a moment what a physical prison looks like, what it is for, and what it accomplishes. I hope you might agree that generally speaking, prisons are physical facilities. They might be made of reinforced concrete, or could even be mud huts or thatched roof villages. Whatever they are made of, two things are always true. They all have a way of keeping the prisoner in and they all have at least one gate. For our purposes though, we must consider a prison from the perspective of an individual. Down at the single prisoner level, the prison consists of typically one room, having walls, a roof or ceiling and one door with a lock on it; we normally call this a cell.

What does the prison do for society? It is thought of as providing a place where those convicted of a crime can be separated from the rest of us as a consequence of their proven violation of the laws of the land. There are, however, other reasons that prisons exist. Some societies place political opponents or psychologically disturbed individuals in jails or institutions, which are "jail substitutes" of course. Other cultures lock away religious dissenters. Whatever the reason or excuse for putting someone in prison the result is always the same. The locked away person is disconnected from his or her family, friends and society.

Emotional prisons are much like their physical counterparts. The big difference is that the physical prison holds the physical person, where the emotional prison holds the Soul.

It is feelings that are the walls and roof of a person's emotional prison. There is also a door, with a lock, a way out, which I'll discuss more in the third book which discusses healing. The emotional prisoner faces the same problem as the physical prisoner, but from a different perspective. It is a problem of disconnection from society, friends and family, while still being part of these groups. This brings me back to the question "What is an emotional prison?"

- **An emotional prison is a place where a person's life is controlled by his or her feelings.**

I know that some people who read this might be saying, and I love this word, poppycock, a very English and a very explicit way of saying that this whole idea of emotional prisons is invalid or not true. This next section is for the doubters.

A very common term in use in the American lexicon is the phrase, "to act out." I find this expression wholly supportive to the idea of emotional prisons. "Acting out" is a shortened version of "acting out of one's emotions." Think about how it is applied in so many ways today:

- A businessman acts out sexual fantasies by going to a prostitute.
- A lonely wife acts out by drinking every afternoon.
- A teenage girl acts out by being promiscuous.
- A teenage boy acts out by joining a gang.

Every person can come up with examples like this. The point is that all over our society people are "acting out." In millions of homes across the country, individual Souls are trapped inside their emotional needs. This whole problem of acting out of emotion has tremendous implications for all of us, as families, as neighborhoods, as cities, as states and as a nation. Some of the implications will resurface throughout the book.

General Spiritual Aspects of Emotional Prisons

At this point I would like to introduce some of the spiritual aspects of emotional prisons. Before I do though, I want to say that any person can be trapped in an emotional prison. One's spiritual condition does not change this truth.

There are some spiritual and theological things to lay out before we can move on. Before we go forward I want to make it clear that I approach this whole subject and the writing of this book from a Christian perspective. I am a person whose has chosen to believe God and His Holy Scriptures, which means that I believe that Jesus Christ is the beginning and end of all things.

4

The First Spiritual Aspect – The Battle

The first spiritual aspect to understanding the importance of emotional prisons is this. There has been a supernatural battle going on since the beginning of time. That is what I call a dramatic statement! I believe it is important to grasp this truth. There are two sides to this battle. One side, to which I belong, is the one true living God, His angels and His followers. The other side is the god of this world (Satan), the fallen angels (who are called demons) and non-followers. Some people don't believe in God, which is their choice, and since they are not for God, they become automatically against Him by default. While it is easy to identify the two sides, it is less easy to figure out what they are fighting over unless you understand Scripture! One explanation to help answer this is in 2 Peter 2:9, which says:

The Lord is not slow about His promise, as some count slowness, but is patient toward you, not wishing for any to perish but for all to come to repentance.

In this verse, God is stating that He doesn't want anybody to perish. In plain language this means that He doesn't want anybody to stay on the opposite side and thereby end up in Hell. The enemy knows this, so it is his greatest delight to cause any human being to end up there.

To be sure that we all are on the same page here I want to expand on this a little further, and not assume that every person reading this has already heard what I am about to say.

At the very start of the Bible, in the book of Genesis, we find what is called "the creation story." Genesis 1:26-27 describe the creation of mankind. It says:

Then God said, "Let Us make man in Our image, according to Our likeness; and let them rule over the fish of the sea and over the birds of the sky and over the cattle and over all the earth, and over every creeping thing that creeps on the earth." God created man in His own image, in the image of God He created him; male and female He created them.

In this passage God tells us that we (humans) are created in His image. What exactly does He mean? Think of all the people you know do they all look the same? No, they have different sizes, shapes and shades. This

5

means that when He says image He is not referring to our physical nature. In support of this we can look at another Scripture verse, John 4:24 in which Jesus Himself says about God:

Jn 4:24 - God is spirit; and those who worship Him must worship in spirit and truth."

I don't see that Jesus mentions that God has any physical characteristics like height, weight or skin color, nor does He mention body parts like arms or legs. After taking away our physical or perishable characteristics, what is left? It is our inner nature or characteristics; He is talking about our Soul, which the Bible says will last forever.

From understanding this we can now come to realization that when God created us in His image He made the most special part of His creation. Just like parents feel toward their children, who are conceived in their image, so God feels about us. Is it any wonder that He loves us so much that He doesn't want to see us perish, that He doesn't want to see us reject Him, and condemn ourselves, through our own choice, to eternal punishment, which we call Hell?

Now I hope we can all agree that the enemy knows this and he knows how much it hurts God to eternally lose a Soul. This is why I say; **The Battle Is For Our Soul!**

How does this fit into emotional prisons? Earlier we talked about what part of us an emotional prison holds. Yes, it is the Soul - the very thing that Satan is fighting God for! The enemy will do all he can to get a human into an emotional prison; it is one of his tactics.

If God's enemy can somehow push a person into an emotional prison, his position is strengthened. This is how it works. For someone that doesn't follow God, it weakens them, it depresses them, and it turns them away from looking for God. A trapped non-believer is almost impossible to reach; they are ruled by their feelings, and they do whatever they can to avoid the conviction of the Holy Spirit. If you've ever talked to someone mired in acting out you know what I mean. For believers or followers it is different. The enemy knows he can't take away God's gift of salvation, but he can try to make life miserable. If he (the enemy) can get us into an emotional prison, we become trapped and ineffective as disciples of Jesus. This is about the best the enemy can do to us from his perspective.

Some of you reading this may have immediately recognized the meaning of this for a Christian. An emotional prison also becomes a spiritual prison. It becomes a place where we will avoid God, and usually indulge in sin. It separates us from the one who truly loves us; the Creator.

The Second Spiritual Aspect – The Soul

Now I want to turn to the second spiritual aspect of emotional prisons which ties in neatly with the first. We identified that the battle is over our Souls. In this part of the book I want to talk about what a Soul is, how it functions and how we are to view it from a biblical perspective. We will also see that when it is malfunctioning, it opens the door to an emotional prison which we sometimes choose to walk through and lock behind us.

Sometimes when one is trying to understand a spiritual thing with great accuracy it is helpful to go back to the original biblical languages. That is the case here. In what we call the Old Testament, God had the writers use a word, "*nephesh*", to describe the Soul. What is interesting about it is that sometimes it is contextually used to mean the heart, the mind or the will (meaning "inner strength"). It appears that God wants us to understand the Soul as being composed of three parts, but with each part being in some way linked to the other and in some circumstances these parts are interchangeable.

Now Jesus, being fully God, knew this when He was asked, "Which is the greatest commandment." His answer was:

Mk 12:30 – And you shall love the Lord your God with all your heart, and with all your soul, and with all your mind and with all your strength.

Some have interpreted this to mean love God with four different parts of your innermost being. In my opinion this is not what Jesus is saying here. He is speaking to a Jewish Scribe, a learned man, and He is emphasizing the message by stating that we are to love God with all our innermost being (Soul) and with each of the innermost parts, heart, mind and strength. Jesus is helping us tremendously here by clearly identifying what the Soul is made up of.

Let us go into a little more detail. Each Soul created by God has three linked parts that have separate roles to play in our lives.

1. The Mind – The inner place that has the most influence over analysis, sorting out and processing which leads to the generation of our thoughts.
2. The Heart – The inner place that has the most influence over the generation and experiencing of our feelings.
3. The Will (sometimes called strength) – The inner place that has the most influence over the making of choices and decisions on our courses of action.

Remember that we have already identified that God says we are created in His image, and that He was speaking about our eternal part, our Soul. Okay, keep following me here. Our Soul is a representation of God Himself, and we know from Scripture that God is three persons in one. Jesus made this clear in the great commission which says:

Mt 28:19 - "Go therefore and make disciples of all the nations, baptizing them in the name of the Father and the Son and the Holy Spirit."

Just as our Soul has three interlinked parts, God Himself has three interlinked persons, and our Soul is made in His image. Let me be very sure to point out that we are not God in any way. We are, though, a reflection of Him, much like a mirror reflects a picture of us, but is not actually us in any way. Since I learned this through study, I have come to a personal understanding that a human Soul and God can be compared as follows:

1. Our Mind seems to be like God the Father, the rational, influential center for thinking about all things.
2. Our Heart is like the Holy Spirit, which helps to guide us like a moral compass through touching our lives through feelings and convictions.
3. Our Will compares with Jesus, the action part of God, through whom choices are made that determine behaviors.

If you've never had a chance to think about how we are created in God's image, what you've just read can be mind blowing. Please remember that this is my opinion which developed over several years of personal study.

Now we come to the place where I use this new understanding to show how when the Soul is not working according to design, we can get stuck in an emotional prison. So that is where we will begin the next chapter.

2

THE MIND

Christianity is the greatest intellectual system the mind of man has ever touched.
Francis Schaeffer.

How does a person get into an Emotional Prison? Generally speaking a person is born into some form of family environment. The early years lay the groundwork for rapid Soul growth of an individual, beginning the process of developing values, beliefs and attitudes. This is followed by the individual being subject to increasingly more external or non-family influence. The final phase of the rapid Soul growth, of a person occurs as that person transitions from being under the family's wings to living independently. After this the person is normally thought of as an adult and the Soul growth slows down. Here in the US we would recognize this as early childhood, childhood, adolescence and then early adulthood.

An individual can actually find themselves in an emotional prison at almost any point in their lives, including early childhood. Generally, as we have imbalances in our emotional lives, such as lots of affection but very little encouragement, we develop behaviors to adjust these imbalances to what we perceive we need. Even a two year old can do it! We'll discuss this in more detail in Chapter 5.

I dated a girl in high school who had a sister a couple of years older than her; we'll call her Christine. Now, this girl wasn't popular, was relatively plain, and didn't ever seem to have friends she would hang out with. When I first met Christine, she was an average sized teenager, and I don't remember her going out on a date even into her early twenties. One of the things that used to happen in their house was the eating of significant amounts of food. The parents both carried significant extra weight and enjoyed their home cooked meals. Looking back I can see that Christine took to eating more than she probably should have. The rejection from her social group at school together with her parents plying us all at mealtime combined to increase her weight significantly. That was my first introduction to comfort food.

Now meet Liz, a high school acquaintance. In our last year in high school she took a lot of time off sick, but never told us what the problem was. We all found out later, and at that time it was a school scandal. A couple of years earlier, at age 15, she had become sexually active. Then in our version of the junior year this really slick jock guy came to our school. She fell for him, and he used her. This went on for months, and then the mystery illnesses started. After the end of our senior school year it came out, that she had had three abortions, forced on her by her parents. The promiscuous behavior she (and he) exhibited finally got her to the point where she allowed herself to get pregnant. Not once, not twice, but three times in one year. She was so trapped in an emotional prison that she first violated normal social values and then tried to pressure or coerce this boy into a deeper relationship than he wanted by becoming pregnant.

What causes people to lock themselves away an emotional prison like Christine and Liz? How does it happen? We are going to explore this last question; how do some of us end up in emotional prisons? To do this some important basic groundwork needs to be covered. In this chapter we will look at the part of the Soul called the Mind. This will be followed in successive chapters with a discussion of the Heart, the Will and then putting it all together.

Our Circumstances are Unique!

Just as surely as we all have our own DNA, our own individual gifts and talents, and also just as surely that we all have different life experiences and grew up in different families, our own path to emotional prison is unique. One of the most well meaning, but condescending, lies we tell one another is this, "I know just how you feel." For years I didn't know or understand why when a caring person said things like that to me I got angry. Then it clicked; they actually have no clue how I feel. It was like they were trying to take something away from me. (If you ever want to say something like this, please stop and think about it first.) The problem is this, every person is on a different life's journey, so how can I know what you might have gone through to get where you are today? It is impossible! The reason I have included this example of misguided actions is to demonstrate that we cannot fully understand or figure out how we, or others, get themselves into an emotional prison.

That is the bad news! The good news is this; there is a process by which people end up in their personal emotional prisons. There are a lot of similarities between the path to emotional prison for a sexaholic and a workaholic. The road to emotional jail for a religious legalist is similar to that of a perfectionist. The rebellious individual got there by a road also traveled by a chemical addict. Starting points, experiences along the way and life's consequences may be different, but the process is always the same.

The Moving Parts of the Soul – Mind, Heart and Will

To begin to explain how we get trapped and thrown into an emotional jail I want to take us back to Chapter 1. In this chapter we talked about how we are "made in the image of God", and we know this to be true, because God Himself said it. We talked about how this meant that our "innermost being" was the part of us that we usually call the Soul. We further talked about how our Soul is similar in functionality to the triune, (meaning three in one) God. Our Soul also has three interlinked and inseparable parts, each having individual functions for our life. Having said all this I am now going to challenge the reader in a deeper understanding of what it means to be "created in His image."

The way our Soul was designed to work is the same way that God Himself works. Our thinking, feeling and choosing of willful actions are intended to be a kind of mirror image of the way God operates. Before anybody thinks that this is claiming too much, let's first discuss what this does not mean.

To add some perspective, let us listen to what God says in Isaiah 55:8-9:

Isa 55:8-9 - "For My thoughts are not your thoughts, nor are your ways My ways," declares the Lord. "For as the heavens are higher than the earth, so are My ways higher than your ways and My thoughts than your thoughts.

God is speaking to all of us here; He is stating that His ways are "higher" than ours. I don't know about you, but I find that easy to acknowledge and accept! What is implied here, and needs to be understood, is that His ways are higher, meaning holier, purer, more accurate, better, superior and so many more things. The part that is absent is this; God does not say that they are different! Did you get that? I believe that God doesn't make errors of judgment or mistakes, He does not say His ways are different, He says they are "higher." He is talking about how our Soul operates! A simplistic comparison might help here. Compare how a peewee football team does things and contrast it to a pro team. Both teams operate under

11

the same basic rules but are the pro team's ways higher? Yes, of course, much higher. I hope I've made my point!

We are now ready to try to figure out where we mess up as fallen people. The starting point is to try to identify how God works. I know that sounds like a challenge, and it is. It might be helpful if I show the reader how this is possible. For non-Christians this might be a new statement, but for believers this is something you have heard before.

"The nature and character of God are revealed through His Scripture"

Knowing and understanding this we can now look at 2 Tim 3:16-17:

All Scripture is inspired by God and profitable for teaching, for reproof, for correction, for training in righteousness; so that the man of God may be adequate, equipped for every good work.

I want us to focus on two points from this well-known Scripture. The first is that it is talking about "all Scripture", the whole Bible. The second is a little subtler. There is a phrase in the middle that says, "for training in righteousness." The Greek word used by the Apostle Paul (the writer of this letter to Timothy) is "**dikaiosune**", which means "equity of character." Paul here is telling his protégé that the whole of God's word will train a person in how to become more like God in the sense of character. It is not the body that has character, it is the Soul. This means that we can learn to think, feel and choose to act more like God by studying Scripture. Put another way, we can learn how God thinks, feels and chooses by studying what He tells us about Himself in His divinely inspired words.

This is how things look to me. God has always existed, His character has been the same forever, and will never change. James 1:17 says this clearly:

Every good thing given and every perfect gift is from above, coming down from the Father of lights, with whom there is no variation or shifting shadow.

This Scripture uses the terms "no variation" and "no shifting shadow", meaning to me that everything we need to know is unchanging. Now it is the moment to uncover what the Bible says about the three moving parts of the Soul.

The Mind – The Center of Thinking

Knowledge

Starting with an understanding that God is unchanging in character, we can look at the way He has indicated He thinks, feels and chooses, remembering He is perfect in all things. What we see is a "blueprint" for how our Soul is supposed to operate. I want to start with the Mind of God by looking at God's servant Job. If there was ever a person that got the pointed end of the stick it was Job. He lost everything except his wife. He lost his material wealth, his physical health, his children, and his friends abandoned him in a relationship sense. When we look at Job in a Bible study, we often focus on suffering and patience, we have all heard the term "patience of Job." I think those things are all true, and there is more!

In Job 38 God finally speaks out! He asks Job the age-old question, and I am paraphrasing here:

Who do you think you are?

God identifies that Job is speaking without knowledge. For us dealing with emotional imprisonment this means that we must consider knowledge, or "knowing stuff" is important in making decisions and taking actions. God thinks, feels and chooses with perfect knowledge, He knows everything; He never shakes his head saying, "I don't know." In fact God spends four chapters (38-41) of this book demonstrating that there is a link between knowledge and actions. By experience we can probably agree that the better we know facts about situations the better our choices of actions will be in trying to deal with those situations.

Understanding

A closely related word to knowledge is "understanding", but it is different in meaning and is treated as a distinct and separate attribute by the Scriptures. Understanding provides a link between knowledge and wisdom, which is discussed below. Understanding is the ability to separate mentally all the facts, emotions and behaviors involved in any given situation; we sometimes call this discernment. God has perfect understanding, and we don't! One of the important things to remember about understanding is that a high level of understanding enables us to function better. Examples of this would be; that we might be able to

13

predict the outcome of a situation or we would be able to provide an employer with higher quality output if we understood better.

Wisdom

The next thing we are to consider is wisdom. Wisdom can be defined as the "ability to discern inner qualities or relationships", which means that it is wisdom that ties together knowledge and understanding for better decision-making. Let us consider an imaginary person, Joe. Now Joe likes to go drinking with his friends, and he is usually restrained, limiting himself to two drinks only. This is because he knows several facts; two drinks will keep him below the legal limit, he can drive normally after two drinks, he has seen his friends do stupid things after two drinks, and it is hard to pick up girls after two drinks. He is being wise. One evening Joe is out with his drinking buddies, and a good looking girl from across the bar buys him a drink and has the bartender take it over. Joe accepts it, thinking that this is going to be his lucky night. The problem is; this will be his third drink. Of course, he has more drinks with the girl after that. I'm sure we would all agree that he made an unwise choice.

What happened here? Well Joe was okay, and discerning about his drinking habits. He connected the consequences of overdoing things and made wise decisions. (I do understand that this is a debatable thing.) But when he was faced with the possibility of feeding another urge, his judgment faltered. He then failed to connect the drink limit he used with the knowledge and understanding of how he acts around pretty girls.

This little story about Joe demonstrates how making wise choices is connected with how much you know and understand. Sometimes wisdom is defined as "applied knowledge." I do like that definition if used in a broad sense. I think, though, that it can be improved upon some by defining it as "applied relevant knowledge." Let me explain why, by using an example where Jesus demonstrates this for us. In the Gospel of Matthew, starting in Chapter 21, Jesus is confronted by the so-called religious leaders of that time. A kind of spiritual sparring went on as these leaders challenged Jesus' authority. Finally, Jesus decides that it is time to get to the point. In Chapter 23, and in my opinion, verse 23 says it best, and I am going to paraphrase.

"You follow the letter of the law, but you miss the intent of it."

In this situation, Jesus is acknowledging that these leaders indeed do know, and do apply the "letter of the law." The problem He sees is very simple. They know, but they don't understand what is important and relevant. Because they don't understand, their application of their knowledge, or put another way, their exercise of their wisdom, falls short of the intent of the law that God gave them. Can you see how knowledge, understanding and wisdom all work together in the Mind?

God has complete and perfect knowledge, He has proven indisputable understanding, and He has infinite wisdom. Any mental choice He makes will be the exact and optimal choice in every circumstance. Any emotional response He has to a situation will be completely appropriate. Any choice of an action He takes will be the exact right thing to do!

There is a Scripture that was spoken by one of God's prophets, Samuel, to the very first king of Israel, Saul. It was when Saul had been disobedient to God, and then God made a decision that Saul was to lose the kingdom, and Samuel was the message bearer. God says, in 1 Samuel 15:29:

Also the Glory of Israel will not lie or change His mind; for He is not a man that He should change His mind.

In this verse, not only does God, called here, "The Glory of Israel", tell us exactly what I wrote above, that He makes a perfect decision, immediately. He also contrasts His decision making with ours.

Let us do what God does and compare that immediate perfect decision-making with how we humans measure up. We don't have perfect knowledge, we can sometimes understand or discern situations and we are able to exhibit wisdom at some level. Our mental decision-making can therefore always be considered suspect. Then when you add in God's point about our innate ability to lie to ourselves and others, our decision-making goes from suspect to highly questionable.

There is some amazingly clear instruction on knowledge, understanding and wisdom found in the book of Proverbs.

Prov 1:7: The fear of the Lord is the beginning of knowledge; Fools despise wisdom and instruction.

Prov 9:10: The fear of the Lord is the beginning of wisdom, and the knowledge of the Holy One is understanding.

It is crystal clear to me. If I want to make better mental judgments, if I want to become more knowledgeable, if I want to make wiser decisions, I ought to "fear the Lord." This "fear" word used here is not the application you might find if you fear a rattlesnake in your back yard. It is the fear of a child for his or her mom and dad; it is a reverential attitude. It is an acknowledgement of how far above us God is in all things, and how absolutely awesome He is. It puts no sense in our minds of a possibility of harm. Do you have a reverential attitude to God? We will be dealing with the significance of this later in the third book, in the section on healing choices.

I want to throw this in here for extra emphasis. Most people know that Solomon was spoken of as the wisest man that ever lived; I even knew that well before I was a Christian. Did you know, however, that that was not the entire truth? Let us look at a very informative verse; it is from the first book of Kings, part of the history of the Jews, chapter 4, verse 29:

Now God gave Solomon wisdom and very great discernment and breadth of mind, like the sand that is on the seashore.

Do you see it? It is the same three Mind attributes that I have been talking about, wisdom, understanding (very great discernment) and knowledge (breadth of mind). Now we can move on to looking at the Heart.

3

THE HEART

A good heart is better than all the heads in the world.
Edward Bulwer-Lytton.

Acting out – possibly the greatest American tradition! Well, it is actually the greatest human tradition. As I've said before, acting out is a short version of acting out of our emotions. When the first man and woman, who we call Adam and Eve, were living in the garden in harmony with God and His creation, they made a decision. Then they disobeyed God, and ate the forbidden fruit. That was the moment that we see mankind beginning to act out. Adam and Eve knew "they were naked" according to Scripture, and "they sewed fig leaves together to cover their loins." Why is this? It is because they felt ashamed, a very powerful feeling! Mankind has been "covering up" in one way or another since that time.

Acting out can be almost a way of life for some people. Consider a friend of mine, Jeremy, not his real name of course. Jeremy is a Senior Vice President of a public company, a regular guy who loves his wife and four children, active in church and enjoys sports. A few years ago one of his golfing buddies introduced him to some news items involving swimsuit pictures of female celebrities on the Internet. From there Jeremy and his buddy navigated to some soft pornography, which is as far as it went - that day. As Jeremy tells it, that is the day his addiction to pornography started. It gradually got worse until he started looking at videos and finally joined in with the action by self-gratification. It was then his wife discovered his problem by catching him the act of masturbation in their home. Jeremy was acting out in sexual way, and was firmly trapped inside an emotional prison.

Emotions such as shame, guilt and anger can be so powerful that they override our ability to make wise and rational choices. My friend Jeremy had let his emotions determine his actions, and he is suffering the consequences even now, which is several years later. What is it about the Heart that is so powerful it can influence the feelings we generate and the choices we make so that we indulge in self-destructive behaviors? I am going to try to explain it in this chapter.

The Heart – The Primary Influencer of Feeling

Much like the Mind, the Heart has three major characteristics, which all tie into how we perceive, from an emotional sense. They are values, beliefs and attitudes. Some might argue that these three things ought to be more associated with the Mind. I am going to reiterate that the Mind and Heart (and Will) are interconnected and inseparable, and so I have a certain sympathy for this argument. My position is that these three "Soul characteristics" have more to do with our **feelings** than our **thinking**, and that is why I connect them to the Heart.

Values

I want to begin with values. Values are a key to determining how a person is going to respond to events or situations. What exactly are values? Where do they come from? Can they change over time? Why are my values different from your values? Why are the values of Americans different from those of Africans or Asians? Why are Christian values so different from Hindu or Moslem values? Are there any values we all have in common? There are so many questions, it is hard to know where to start.

I think a good place to start is by understanding what a value is. Value is used many ways in the English language. We use it to describe monetary, economic, musical and scientific quantities; we use it to indicate importance of certain actions like being able to perform surgery or hit a ball well. None of these describes a value found in somebody's Soul. The definition I found in Webster's dictionary is the one I will use:

"Value – A principle, standard or quality regarded as worthwhile or desirable."

Values have meaning to the person who **owns** them. Furthermore every human being that has existed or will exist has values. This meaning or sense of worth we give to something or someone provides us with an emotional connection. For example, if you adore classical music, you would value going to the symphony, and you might experience pleasant feelings like peace and happiness when listening to it. However, if you had to go to a rock music concert, you might experience negative feelings, like chaos or disconnection. We have to understand that we **own** our values, they belong to us. We must all acknowledge that our values have the ability to influence how we think and choose, as well as how we feel. And this is the source of a problem, and as we will discover later, it is part of the reason we find ourselves in an emotional prison.

I have actually done this in a teaching session. I asked the class to write down their top twenty values, and to a person they could not do it, including me! That did not surprise me, because it is not something we normally think about. When I reflect on how powerful values are and compare that to how little energy is put into knowing what we stand for, I grimace. The reason we don't generally identify our values well is that it is too hard and can feel very unsafe. Let me try to demonstrate this.

We can probably all identify a few things that fit our definition of a value. As you are reading this stop for sixty seconds and pinpoint a few in your own life. That wasn't too hard was it? Then as you get to the fifth or sixth value and then beyond, you begin to realize that you are not so sure of what they are. In fact you might even find it difficult to connect some of your values with your beliefs, which I cover later in this chapter. When I did this for myself, I found it really unsettling, and hard. Then there is also the issue of unsafeness.

I want to demonstrate how having a value can feel unsafe. I am going to use one of the hot button issues of our day, abortion. Let us say you have a value that says, "I value life, and I believe it begins at conception." This means you are likely to believe that abortion is morally wrong. If you went to most (it is unfortunate that I can't say all) churches, and stood up and stated your value, you would get agreement, and feel safe. If, however, you went to a Planned Parenthood convention (Planned Parenthood, to my understanding, is the largest provider of abortions in the United States) you would most likely get booed off the stage and possibly thrown out, and you would certainly feel unsafe. It is this sense of not feeling safe that sometimes stops us speaking up for our values.

I have often demonstrated the ability to say I have one value about a subject, and yet act like I have a different value This is the sin called hypocrisy, and I know I'm not alone! Our whole society does it. How many times have we heard the term "family values" come out of a politician's mouth, which is then followed by some form of scandal? This example of the abuse of the word "values" brings me to my next point about values, where do they come from?

The broad answer is of course, the world! What does this mean? It means that most of us get the majority of our values from our environment, from every person we know, every TV show we watch and every book, magazine or newspaper we read. Think about it - our parents tried to give us values, and some of them stuck, but where did they get their values from? We are absolutely bombarded with "take my value and make it your own" messages every day. Even the church does it, although their motivation is usually purer than Madison Avenue's. It is my contention that these worldly values we pick up lead to longer term Soul issues and help push us into an emotional prison.

It is now time to bring up God again. What does He say, what are His values? What does he want us to value, and why? Jesus makes the single most important value statement ever made in history. In the first three gospels, the books of Matthew, Mark and Luke, an encounter is highlighted between Jesus and the Jewish religious leaders, and they try to trick Him with a question. Let us look at what He says, and this is what I just called the greatest value statement ever, it is found in Matthew 22:36-40.

"Teacher, which is the great commandment in the Law?" And He said to him, " 'YOU SHALL LOVE THE LORD YOUR GOD WITH ALL YOUR HEART, AND WITH ALL YOUR SOUL, AND WITH ALL YOUR MIND.' "This is the great and foremost commandment. "The second is like it, 'YOU SHALL LOVE YOUR NEIGHBOR AS YOURSELF.' " On these two commandments depend the whole Law and the Prophets."

In a nutshell here it is; Love God, Love Yourself, Love Others. In that order and priority. I included verse 40, which says, **"On these two commandments depend the whole Law and the Prophets."** We must not miss this point. Jesus gave us the values, and He added the extra point to tell the Jews, and now us through the written word, that everything depends on these values. Don't be confused by the word "commandment." Jesus was telling us to value God above all things, then value ourselves and others after that, and demonstrate it through love.

Every choice we make, everything we think, and everything we feel can be tested against these three values. Take your mind back to what you have done over the last twenty-four hours - have you been meeting the standard set by these values? I address this in an in-depth way with Healing Choice Number Seven in the third "Emotional Prisons" book.

Not only does God's word, the Bible, give us these three values, but it also has other values spelled out for more detail. Examples of this are found throughout the Bible; the best illustration is recorded for us in Exodus 20:1-17, in what is traditionally called the "Ten Commandments." Take a look at them again sometime and think of them as the ten values.

A challenge for all of us is to search our Hearts and look to see if we are using the values God Himself has written down for us, or do we use something else. There is a wonderful Psalm that looks at the whole subject of are we using God's values or using values from worldly sources. In Psalm 119 we find an extensive look at the results of using ungodly values, and how because of that our lives are less rich and full than they could be. It seems to me that if we could all run our lives with God's values screening our thoughts, feelings and actions, we might not end up in emotional prisons. I want to quote just one verse from Psalm 119, it is verse 105:

Your word is a lamp to my feet, and a light to my path.

This verse captures what I'm saying, God's word, which contains God's values, shows you the right road to travel on.

Beliefs

Next I am going to focus our attention on the subject of "beliefs." What is a belief? Again I turn to Webster's dictionary:

A belief is "A mental acceptance of, or conviction in, the truth or actuality of something."

That is quite a mouthful. Did you notice that the definition used the phrase "mental acceptance" and earlier I said beliefs had more to do with emotion than thoughts? Again, I will admit that I have a minor sympathy with it being a "mental acceptance", but let me explain why I'm sticking with my view that it is a matter of the Heart.

When someone says, "I believe", he or she is making a statement where they "know" something, but don't have a one hundred percent certainty. To make a statement of belief in something there has to be an emotional buy-in. The person making the statement has to have a positive feeling in their Soul about the statement. Think about it. Are you going to make a statement of belief about something you have a negative feeling about? You are not! Either way, whether you believe or not believe something, it is the emotion that primarily finalizes your decision; it doesn't come through the path of knowledge, understanding and wisdom.

In fact, beliefs can be very irrational. Take the group that is known as "truthers" as an example. This group believes that the US government was behind the 9/11 attacks. They believe it despite all the evidence of their own eyes, the science, the attackers' videotapes and much more proof. Why do they believe this lie? They come at the subject from an emotional perspective. Some of them fantasize about conspiracy theories, others hate the United States and want to blame them for everything bad in the world, and still others can't connect peace loving religious people with such atrocities. Did you notice how these amorphous groups are believing the lie through their emotions? They fantasize, blame and disconnect.

It seems to me that when we move from irrefutable knowledge, which is regulated by the Mind, to belief, by adding irrational or subjective components to pieces of information, we are connecting to, and are regulated by, the Heart. I wonder what God might say about this? The answer to this is found in the book of Romans:

Rom 10:9-10 - That if you confess with your mouth Jesus as Lord, and believe in your heart that God raised Him from the dead, you will be saved; for with the heart a person believes, resulting in righteousness, and with the mouth he confesses, resulting in salvation.

Right there it says it. In verse 9 it says, "believe in your heart" and in verse 10 it says, "for with the heart a person believes." For those of you that ever wondered about what it takes to be a Christian, the writer, Paul the Apostle, tells us in plain English. (In the interests of accuracy, Paul actually wrote this book in Greek.) The point is, there are two things for us to do:

- **Confess out loud that Jesus is Lord.**
- **Believe in your Heart that He was raised from the dead.**

If you have never done those two things and want to now, go ahead, it is between you and God, and it is solely your choice.

For those who may have chosen to do what we call "accepting Christ", the next thing to be done is for you to plug yourself into a church that believes the Bible is the inspired word of God. They will be able to take it from there, and will help you go from being young in the faith to becoming more mature.

I think that we have established that beliefs are a Heart function. The only problem we now must face is where do the beliefs come from. If we get our beliefs from our family, friends, TV, newspapers, magazines or the internet, we are going to run into a totally self-centered set of people. They will put their views forward as facts, not opinions, and we can all be fooled into developing beliefs that won't stand up to real truth. The only source we can rely on is God Himself, which implies that we must have a relationship with Him through talking with Him, prayer, and through studying His word, the Bible. As Jesus said about Himself in John 14:6:

Jesus said to him, "I am the way, and the truth, and the life; no one comes to the Father but through Me.

If you want the truth go to Jesus!

Attitudes

Attitudes are next. What is an attitude? Webster's says this:

"An attitude is a state of mind or feeling."

If one looks up the word "attitude" in a thesaurus, other similar words pop up like, approach, outlook, manner, stance, posture, feelings, pose or bearing. Again, we run into the question of whether this characteristic relates to the Mind or Heart, and again I say the Heart, and this is why. Have you ever noticed that our approach to something can vary from day to day? This is because even when we are faced with the same situation, our feelings change when we look at it. Who among us has not woken up to an alarm in the morning with a "up and at them" attitude one day and an "I don't want to get up" the next. What is so different? The facts are the same each day It is our feelings that govern our attitude about getting up.

I tend to think of my attitudes as being "inclinations of the heart", which is why I like synonyms for attitude such as "posture", "pose" or "bearing." You might agree with me on this when you consider how some of the people you know deal with life. Some of them have an attitude, which can be either positive or negative. When they feel negatively toward something, how do you deal with them? For most of us, avoidance works well, which means nobody benefits and typically nothing gets done. Think of a time a co-worker came in with an angry attitude, did you spend a moment asking how the day was going, or did you ask them if they watched the game last night? No, you left them alone as much as possible; you could see that their Heart was not inclined in a positive position.

Contrast that with a co-worker who comes in whistling or smiling, having no trace of grumpiness in their voice. You, unless you are the one with the less than stellar attitude, want to begin interacting and getting on with things. Work goes so much better, you are both more productive, and life seems better. A glad attitude is the sign of a positively inclined heart. That makes me think of the movie "Pollyanna" about the little girl who was taught by her father to always have a glad attitude. Do you remember that by the end of the movie she had so transformed the town that the people changed the name of the town to Gladtown? Attitudes come from the Heart and have a significant influence on how we conduct ourselves, and on how people perceive us.

Does God have anything to say about attitude? He does; I just enjoy the absolute direct and simple way He communicates about this. He says:

Jer 12:3 - But You know me, O Lord; You see me; And You examine my heart's attitude toward You.

God states here that He knows us, sees us, and examines the attitude in the Heart. Have you ever thought about having your attitudes examined? It is really a scary proposition. What if your spouse or co-worker knew exactly what attitude you had toward them at every moment? It could produce some interesting conversations!

Tying Them Together

I want to tie the three "Heart" characteristics together now.

Is there a better place to demonstrate this than in the world of politics? If you tend to have values that focus on things like social justice, pacifism, globalism, and wealth distribution then you tend to develop certain beliefs. You might believe in extensive welfare programs, probation versus incarceration, staying out of wars, working closely with global organizations like the United Nations, and higher taxes for wealthier people or corporations. This set of beliefs which originate from your values then leads you to have attitudes such as being pro big government,

24

for lower prison sentences for minor crimes, small military, being agreeable to the jurisdiction of worldwide courts and a "tax the rich" posture. In the United States you would be known as liberal or progressive.

The other side, which we usually call conservative, has a different set of values, beliefs and attitudes. They might value individualism, peace through strength, national sovereignty and meritocracy. The beliefs would then be small welfare programs, strong or large military, national law instead of international law and keeping what you earn. The attitudes that could go with these beliefs are small government, pro military, anti-United Nations and lower individual tax rates.

It is fairly easy to see the links between values, beliefs and attitudes in the world of politics, and it is also easy to see something else. That is how when principled people of either side get entangled in these things they can be blinded to other more important values. It comes out as name-calling, anarchistic behavior, acrimonious talk in Congress, lying about facts that don't support your views and much more. Some of the people involved in politics who do these things are so emotionally bound up in their beliefs that they get trapped into an emotional prison of their own making.

Does God say anything about this linkage? He does:

Ecc 11:9 - Rejoice, young man, during your childhood, and let your heart be pleasant during the days of young manhood. And follow the impulses of your heart and the desires of your eyes. Yet know that God will bring you to judgment for all these things.

In this scripture God links "let your heart be pleasant," which is attitude, with "follow the impulses of your heart," which is beliefs, and finally "desires of your eyes," which is values. The problem is that God then says through Solomon's words, and I paraphrase it, **"you will have to answer for it**." When I read this I get the sense that we are being warned about following our emotions, because they are going to get us into trouble. That, of course, is what I am writing about in this book, how our emotions can get us into a prison.

God actually goes a little further in helping us understand what we ought to consider when thinking about our own Hearts. Look at what He says:

Jer 17:9 - The heart is more deceitful than all else, and is desperately sick; who can understand it?

If we can assume that God is speaking the truth, which I do, then we all ought to examine our values, beliefs and attitudes throughout our lives. If they don't match up to God's standards then we are going to lead a lesser life than we could, and for some this means a falling into an emotional prison.

4

THE WILL

The will is the strong blind man who carries on his shoulders the lame man who can see.
Arthur Schopenhauer

Have you ever found yourself doing something that you know you don't want to do? Maybe it is eating that extra doughnut at the office, or looking at that pretty girl a little too long, or perhaps you have flirted with a co-worker again. We all seem to do things that we know are just plain wrong, or that will end up harming us. This is where the Will is working in concert with some misleading feelings and ignoring wisdom that is stored in our Mind. Consider a co-worker I had back in the eighties, we'll call her Jenny.

Jenny was an attractive young girl, recently out of college and on her first real post-graduation job. She had enjoyed her time at university, made it through with a decent GPA, and was somewhat of a party person. The adjustment to the real world didn't seem to go well, and she started to put on weight after only a few months. Her relationships seemed to be short, ending after only a few weeks, and she often arrive at work with a hangover. We all knew what was going on because she would chatter on and on about seemingly everything. After about a year her stories started to turn into tales of rejection and loneliness. Not long after her parents made her quit her job with us and go back to live at home. We never knew what eventually happened to her.

Jenny couldn't say no. She couldn't say no to men, to alcohol, and to food, her parents obviously seemed to realize it, and took her back under their wing. Knowing what I know now I can see that Jenny had a dysfunctional Soul. Her emotions ran her life and she couldn't exert her personal will power to stop doing things that hurt her. Her emotional prisons, whatever they were, were slowly and surely killing her.

The Will – The Center of Action

The Will! Much has been said and written about this seemingly mysterious part of our Soul. Theologians and philosophers fuss about

27

things like, "Determinism", "Compatibilism" and "Metaphysical Libertarianism." In fact there are many attempts to explain issues surrounding the concept of "free will." A theory that provides even a reasonable fit to how humans exercise their free will seems to elude them all. One of the problems which I perceive is that these theories do not consider and attempt to understand the Will in the proper context. The Will is part of the Soul and cannot be considered as separated from the Mind and Heart. The Will would not function without the other parts of the Soul!

Just like the Mind and Heart, the Will has unique characteristics, and also like the Mind and Heart it has three vital functions. These are choice, control and gateway. If we are to get a grip on our understanding of what an emotional prison is and how it gets established we must become very cognizant of the role of the Will. The Will is very important to every person alive, although they may not realize it. The only thing we can observe about another person is the "fruit of the Will." By this I mean the actions a person takes.

Fruit of the Will

I hope that every reader can agree with what I am about to say. Nobody can read another person's Mind. I'll go one step further: Nobody can see into another person's Heart. What is true is that we all believe we can make a good guess at the state of someone's Heart or what they may be thinking. We must admit, though, that we cannot be sure of what is in the Mind or Heart of another person. Where does that leave us? With the outward actions, or what I called earlier the fruit of the Will.

We base our opinions of others on two things; what we observe that they do, and what others tell us that they have observed the subject person doing. When a person outwardly exercises their Will they do something. It is some form of action. It could be so many different things, from quietly standing still to killing another person. It could be offering words of appreciation to putting down a co-worker. They are all actions, and all actions give us a piece of information about the individual doing the acting.

A word exercise may be useful here. What if you hear about one of your neighbors on the nightly news, and that he has killed a man at his office. The police are parked ten deep on your street, with red and blue lights, sirens, bullhorns, news crews, the whole thing. What are you to think?

28

Maybe it is, "I live near a murderer" or "I wonder if he shot him" or many other thoughts. You could easily be led to form a judgment of what might have been in this neighbor's Mind and Heart, or at least speculated on it.

In the morning, with the police still blocking the street, you catch the morning news. Your neighbor had actually tackled an angry ex-employee who had come in to shoot the boss. In the scuffle, the gun accidentally went off, killing the ex-employee. The neighbor had saved the bosses life! Does your analysis of your neighbor's Mind and Heart change? Of course it does! You now have more information on the behavior (outward action of the Will) of the neighbor. This example also serves to remind us all about making hasty judgments, which I have done many times!

I like to believe that the Will can be thought of as "the window of the Soul", and as we now get familiar with what is does, and how it works, we'll see if this is a reasonable description. I wrote earlier that the Will has three characteristics, choice, control and gateway, and now it is time to look at these individually.

Choice

Choice, choice, choice! Sometimes I get a little sick of choice. When my wife has me go to the store, she gives me a list, because she knows me well. On this list sometimes I find something like "bran flakes." Do you how many types of "bran flakes" there are? In the store I last went to there were 22 different choices! I think I'm quick at making simple decisions, but this one always gets me shaking my head, and takes about 5 minutes! Too much choice! What exactly is choice, what is the definition? As usual I turn to my trusty Webster's dictionary, where is says:

"Choice is the power, right or liberty to choose."

I like that definition, because it covers all three aspects of the function of the Will called choice. The Will has the power, right and freedom to choose a course of action for the Soul.

The power we are talking about here is the ability and capacity to perform the internal action of choice. This choice could be conscious or sub-conscious. The right involved in the activities of choice is that the Will is the right place for choice to occur; actually it is the only place! More on this later. Freedom is, of course, the condition of being free of constraints.

The next question for me is, how does this fit into what we have already looked at, meaning the Heart and the Mind? Let's remember the characteristics of the Heart and Mind. The Mind, has "knowledge, understanding and wisdom", the Heart has "values, beliefs and attitudes." It is the Will that combines all these things and produces a choice. It is really that simple!

As has been my pattern, I would like to look at what God says on this subject. An interesting question that I have reflected on in the past, and eventually came to a conclusion on is this, "Did Adam and Eve have a choice?" Which said another way is "Were humans designed with a freedom, right and power to choose?" We need to consider what happened "in the beginning." I'm going to look at the book of Genesis 2:16-17:

The Lord God commanded the man, saying, "From any tree of the garden you may eat freely; but from the tree of the knowledge of good and evil you shall not eat, for in the day that you eat from it you will surely die."

This is the first recorded instruction God gave to mankind. From it we can see that "the man", who is later called Adam, is given the freedom to choose. This verse says to me, "You can choose to eat anything you see, but don't choose the tree of knowledge, it will kill you." God, by His own design, has given Adam, and consequently all who follow, the freedom to choose, the ability or power to choose, and the unrestrained right to choose. This ability, right and freedom to choose includes, as was the case with Adam, choices that might harm us. So from the very creation of the first person and up to now, our Soul has always had this characteristic.

Control

I don't think many people would disagree with the fact that we are free to choose, but they might have to think twice about this next one. Our Will has the characteristic of being able to control how we behave!

What is control? Let us ask Mr. Webster:

"Control is the authority or ability to regulate, direct or influence."

When we think about control, what comes to our mind? Things like laws, or not losing our temper, or maybe how our "control freak" parents treated us when we were kids. There are many things we could consider, but the one that is relevant here is the one we might call "control of ourselves."

Self-control, or lack of it, comes as a direct result of a choice we make. From the discussion above about choice we know that choosing is an activity of the Will. So it is with self-control. Not only can we choose what our action is to be, we can choose how much of it we are going to have, and how we are going to display it.

We tend to think of self-control as keeping our emotions in check, or not doing too much of something (such as drinking alcohol, or gorging on food), but it is more than that. It also includes what we allow to influence us. It is important to understand this, because as we will see later, what goes into our Heart and Mind can help to push us into an emotional prison. As an example, think about whom you associate with, which is the same thing as whom you allow to influence you in an interpersonal way. If you choose to hang out with drug addicts there is a really good chance that you might end up saying, "yes" to drugs yourself.

When I talk about self-control, I am primarily considering that this only applies to individuals who have responsibility for their own decisions, because they can control their actions. There are groups of people who may not exactly fit this mold; these would include people who would be evaluated by the appropriate person as not being of sound mind. It would also include children, although I am not willing to let them off the hook of accountability too easily; they can learn to develop better personal control, as they get older.

Consider the person; we'll call him Bob, who, in response to a situation, quickly blurts out an angry remark. It may or may not be justified, but the rightness or wrongness is not at issue here. The issue is, was the response a self-controlled one? We have all done something like that, and know people that always seem to act like that. What is happening inside of the Soul of somebody who does this?

The anger coming out in a seemingly uncontrolled outburst is the product of a process that is simple to explain, but is probably complex in its detail. Bob has stored up years of experience, he has accumulated knowledge, developed understanding and wisdom. His values, beliefs and attitudes have been challenged by this event. He has made what I call an "automated response", which put another way is his "habitual choice" to be angry, and he is letting it out with a lack of self-control. He has probably done this many, many, times, and it, generally speaking, results in him getting some form of feedback, which supports his reactions and confirms that his response is "right." The problem is, he is out of control!

From the example of Bob, we can see that the characteristics of the Soul work together to get to the point of action. Bob's Will chose what to do, the choice was followed by another decision to let out his response, and this is the control decision. I hope you can see that control follows choice in the way the Soul works. Although I have used anger here, Bob's response could have been many other things. It could include messages of frustration or pain; it might also have been silence or tears.

There is a big "what-if." What if Bob had decided to choose anger as he normally would, but not expressed himself verbally? What if he chose anger and chose to think about it. His Soul would have the opportunity to work in a more controlled way. He could have reached down into the depths of his Mind and remembered wise things he had not considered recently. He could have seen how blurting words out didn't line up with his internal beliefs about using his tongue wisely. He could have had a chance to exercise self-control!

I have tried to show the reader how, using the example of angry Bob, control is a function of the Will, and how it flows from the whole of the Soul working in unison through choice and into some form of action. Bob's case showed the all too familiar example of a person seemingly "reacting" to a situation, without consideration of all factors. He didn't give himself an opportunity to be thoughtful and apply some understanding and wisdom to the situation. He didn't allow himself time to process his emotional response internally within his Soul, before rushing to action. Consequently his choice of response was poor, and that was followed by an equally poor illustration of lack of self-control.

What Might God Say?

If Bob had given God a chance to communicate with him on how he, Bob, lets his self-control go, what would God talk about? I think He might say something like this. "Bob, check out my word, you know, the Bible. I have put a couple of things in there about self-control - look them up and think about what I've said." Upon checking it out, Bob would discover a couple of things:

Stop depriving one another, except by agreement for a time, so that you may devote yourselves to prayer, and come together again so that Satan will not tempt you because of your lack of self-control.

This is from 1 Corinthians 7:5. It is dealing with the subject of sexual relations between a husband and wife, and addresses the subject of denying one another this physical aspect of marriage. The Apostle Paul is pointing out that lack of self-control puts a person in the position of easily being tempted to do something wrong. In this verse he is looking at what might happen in a marriage, but he is clearly stating the practical result of a lack of self-control, which is vulnerability to temptation.

In the second verse that God may direct Bob to look at, we see how God places self-control in the position of being a virtue. Let us look at 2 Peter 1:5-8:

Now for this very reason also, applying all diligence, in your faith supply moral excellence, and in your moral excellence, knowledge, and in your knowledge, self-control, and in your self-control, perseverance, and in your perseverance, godliness, and in your godliness, brotherly kindness, and in your brotherly kindness, love. For if these qualities are yours and are increasing, they render you neither useless nor unfruitful in the true knowledge of our Lord Jesus Christ.

This is the positive side of self-control. This section of Scripture shows us that self-control is part of a list of positive attributes that result in a person becoming "fruitful." It may seem intuitively obvious that lack of self-control is bad for us, and having self-control is good, but the Word of God lays it out well, so there is no doubt where God stands. In fact, when we study the Scriptural view of self-control a little deeper, we find that God says it is a "fruit of the Spirit." He says this in Galatians 5:22-23:

But the fruit of the Spirit is love, joy, peace, patience, kindness, goodness, faithfulness, gentleness, self-control; against such things there is no law.

This is where we have to develop a good understanding of God's statement. He is saying that self-control is part of the "fruit of the Spirit", which means it is a result of us having the Holy Spirit inside our Souls. For the non-Christian, this can be difficult to comprehend. I'll try to help though. When a person becomes a Christian, they are said to receive the Holy Spirit into their Hearts. In the context of self-control, it is God who enables us to be this way (self-controlled), through His Spirit. People who are not Christian but demonstrate what looks like self-control are actually only showing a limited form of self-control called self-restraint.

The difference is straightforward. When one has the Holy Spirit inside their Heart, they have access to what is normally thought of as the power of God. For the Christian, self-control comes as a result of allowing God to help us deal with our situations. As a Christian matures, he or she becomes more reliant on God, and therefore bears (demonstrates) the "fruit" called self-control in their lives. For the non-Christian, it is different; they rely on their own internal power to control their actions. This is why I have suggested it is a limited form of self-control, and called it self-restraint.

Gateway

We have now looked at the Mind, Heart and some of the function of the Will, and is time to address what I think is the single most important aspect of the Soul. The characteristic of the Will, which I have called the "gateway."

I alluded to this "gateway" characteristic earlier when I talked about what we allow to influence us, and offered the example of hanging out with drug addicts. We have come to understand how our Will is the part of the Soul responsible for making choices on how we are going to behave. We also recognize that we have control over our choice, and that this means we determine the "size and shape" of how we are responding. Now we come to the point where we decide if and when we let our response out. I have called this the "gateway" decision because we have to open up the "gateway" of our Soul, which is in the Will, to let out our controlled choice.

Now we are at the point where the significance of the gateway needs to be clearly stated. Have you ever noticed that when you open the front door of your house, objects can go out, or objects can come in? I know I'm stating the obvious when I say that, but that is the way it is with the Soul. This gateway can be opened to let out choices, and it can also be opened to let in choices. This has tremendous repercussions for how we ought to consider living our lives, and I want to explore these for a while.

First, let's look at opening our gateway in the context of allowing something out. I am going to assume that a controlled choice has been made and we are ready to implement it. For this choice to happen we have

34

to let it out of the gate. The gate is opened and it happens. Simple, right? Yes and no.

What if we are dealing with the automated response I used earlier? Part of this automation is the Soul mechanically opening the gateway without any consideration of the outcome. It is as though we gave some little guy a remote control that hits "open" when a choice is made by our Will. There is no kind of discriminating decision made on whether to open the gateway or not. We simply, let it all out! I hope you would all agree with me when I say that this is no way to conduct ourselves.

Just like the decision of choice, and the decision of control, we can decide when to open our gate to let something out, and we ought to do it with appropriate consideration. The Soul is designed to work within itself to come to the best choice we can make and in a controlled fashion, open the gate and let it out. The decision to open the gateway to outside the Soul is the final and irreversible step in an internal action we take. Once out of the gate the choice is public!

I would like to take a look at some of our internal actions and how they relate to the gateway. Let's say we observe something, maybe an argument between two people we don't even know. We might think about what we are seeing, we might feel something, and we most likely might choose to do nothing, so we decide that the gate stays shut. What if though, it is right in front of us at the office, between two co-workers? We almost certainly will think and feel something, we will call on our knowledge of the two people, and get in touch with how we feel about them, and we will choose to do something. It may be to not involve ourself, in which case the gateway slowly opens, and causes us to continue watching or we leave. It could also be to join in, so our gateway opens and we start putting in our 10 cents worth. It could be that we decide to intervene, therefore our gateway quickly opens and we speak or physically get in the way.

From this example we can see that the opening of a gateway is dependent on what choice of response the Will makes. Well-considered responses lead us to make good decisions on whether or not to open the gateway, and how urgently it needs to be opened. Ill-considered responses lead to other decisions on the opening of gateways. These other decisions could be things like premature opening, or not opening when it should be, or possibly even opening the gateway too late. The point here is that the gateway inside all of us only works well in implementing our choices when the whole Soul is involved.

Letting Things In

Now I want to come to the second aspect of gateway opening. What happens when we open this gate to allow things in? We are influenced! Just think of how simply true that is. We are all influenced in many ways each day. We open our gateway to the outside when we talk to others, when we read books, magazines or newspapers, when we watch TV or movies, and perhaps the single most important one in our generation, when we log on to the internet. I believe more human effort goes into influencing others, or the attempt to get through the gateway of others, than any other activity. Add up all the money and time spent in advertising, writing books (just like me, ha!) magazines and newspapers, setting up political organizations, web sites and more. It is our very Souls these people are after, they are trying to determine, at some level, what we think, how we feel, and what we choose. I will leave it to you to determine the motivation behind all this activity.

As an individual I have an enormous responsibility to myself, for the sake of my personal integrity, to be very careful about what I let into my Soul through the gateway. I gave an example earlier about hanging out with drug addicts. What if I started to do that? How would it impact me, and more importantly, my family? Asking that question brings clarity to this issue. If we let lies, bad habits, impure thoughts, self-centered desires and other negative attitudes into our Souls through the gateway, what is going to happen to our ability to make good choices? More than anything about this one subject, I hope that all parents think about how this line of thinking impacts their children. We have to protect those immature Souls, and I'm not sure we are doing it as a nation.

I wonder if God has anything to say about all these things?

To begin developing an understanding of what the "Will" of God looks like I would like to take us back into Chapter One. In that chapter we recognized that through Scripture God identifies Himself as having what we call "three persons." These are the Father, the Holy Spirit and the Son (Jesus). We also came to an understanding that our Souls are made in the image of God. This, in turn, allowed us to see that the three parts of the Soul matched up with the three persons of God, in the following way:

- God the Father is represented as our "Mind."
- God the Holy Spirit is represented as our "Heart."
- God the Son is represented as our "Will."

Looking at the question, "What does God's "Will" look like?" is now simple to answer. It looks like God the Son, Jesus. Let us now look and see the evidence supporting this statement found in the Scriptures. Before looking at some verses, let us be sure to remember the three characteristics of the Will we acknowledged earlier. These are choice, control and gateway.

For me, Scripture has an amazing way of revealing things. I can read something, and understand it well. Then a while later I can read it again, and it means more, I understand more. I have come to believe that this is the primary way God speaks to me, through Scriptural revelation. It is that very thing that happened with this next verse. Let's read from the gospel of Matthew (It is also found in Lk 10:22):

Mt 11:27 - All things have been handed over to Me by My Father; and no one knows the Son except the Father; nor does anyone know the Father except the Son, and anyone to whom the Son wills to reveal Him.

This is Jesus speaking in His role as a man, and He says that God the Father has put Him, Jesus, in charge of everything. That is the way I understood it originally, and I thought about it strictly in the context of the verses that followed. Now I see it differently.

Now I see choice, control and gateway! God the Father has delegated something to God the Son (Jesus) and that is that Jesus is to handle everything. Jesus therefore has the responsibility, and the authority, to do all things. He has the power (of God), the right (from God) and the freedom (in God) to choose to do whatever He wants. In the second part of the verse Jesus declares that nobody knows the Father unless He, Jesus, allows it. This is control. It further states that Jesus, must "reveal" the Father; this is what I have called the "gateway." It is through Jesus that we can come to meet God the Father. It is only when Jesus opens the gate for us that we can begin to connect with God in a personal way.

There is a Scripture that we Christians like to point to which emphasizes how we can be made right with God, sometimes called being "saved." This Scripture is found in John 14:6. Jesus is answering a question from

Thomas, one of His closest disciples, about how they are going to be able to follow Him after He leaves. This is what Jesus says:

Jesus said to him, "I am the way, and the truth, and the life; no one comes to the Father but through Me.

This is such a rich and powerful verse, from which many sermons could be preached, but I'm going to keep my comments short. In this verse, we can see that Jesus attributes three characteristics to Himself, the "way", "truth" and "life." While I believe He is the "truth", meaning the only absolute certainty that exists (He is speaking as God), and I believe He is the "life", meaning the grantor of everlasting life with God, my main focus here is the "way."

Jesus is the "way." The explanation of this expression I first learned, which is the traditional view, was that believing in Jesus is the only "way" to get into Heaven. At the end of this verse He says, "No one comes to the Father but through Me", which seems to support the view of Jesus being the "only way." I have come to look at this verse differently over the last few years.

I struggled with trying to understand how people who knew God before the time of Jesus got into Heaven. There was Biblical evidence that they were there, but they didn't know Jesus, so how did they get in? The explanation was always something like "they looked forward to the cross" or "they believed in a savior to come." For me, as I have said, this was a struggle to believe. Then as I studied and thought about it differently it came to me. When Jesus talks about Himself as the "way", He means he is the gateway to God!

Just like He says, He is the "way", it is Jesus who opens the gateway for us to "come to the Father", and it is Jesus who opened the gateway to Heaven for all those who preceded us "believing" God. I want us all to recognize that I didn't say, "believing in" God. Even some of God's enemies "believe in" God! This distinction makes an enormous difference in our attempts to get out of an emotional prison, which will be covered later in the last of the three Emotional Prisons books.

I hope you can see that Jesus is indeed the very "Will" of God, and that He is in control of the "gateway" to many things of importance. I'm going to list a few:

- The Father, and the Holy Spirit
- Everlasting Life
- Heaven
- Freedom
- Healing
- Safety

The Relationship of God's Will with Our Will

I know I've put you through a lot of dialogue, thoughts and ideas here, I hope you will allow one last major point to be made. This is an introductory discussion on the relationship between God's Will and our Will.

Have you ever stayed in one of those hotel rooms where there is an adjoining room and you have a door between you? If you think about it though, there are always actually two doors! Each room occupant has to open their door for both sides to have access. These doors allow back and forth movement to occur without having to go out of the room into the open space outside. We call that privacy. It can also be thought of as safety. When we go on a road trip with our kids, we might get two adjoining rooms with this type of doorway. We are then able to keep our kids safe from the outside world more easily.

So it is with God and us. He has a gateway, and He opens and closes it as He desires, and He is our heavenly parent. We are created in His image with our own gateway, which we can open and close as we wish. If we choose to put our gateway next to His, we have created adjoining rooms! At the moment we do this we have aligned ourselves with God, but our door is closed. Then when we choose to open it and invite Him in, we are said to be asking Jesus to come into our hearts. The first time we do this is sometimes called "the moment of salvation", or by some as "being born again." The whole point is this: the lining up and opening of our gateway with God's gateway requires us to choose to do it, we have control of the whole process and we open up when we wish to.

This event I have described is the beginning of our Christianity. From that moment on we will always be Christians, nothing can change that, but there is still a lingering problem. We still carry our individual personality, experiences and character defects around. At the moment of salvation we are all still governed by our lack of knowledge, understanding and wisdom, as well as our worldly values, beliefs and attitudes. Only one thing has actually changed, and that is our acceptance that God is God and we are not. If we are in an emotional prison before accepting God, then we still are I one after this special moment. However, we have the hope of God in us, and that is where escape from an emotional prison begins.

Below there is pictorial representation of the Soul with all the component parts I have been discussing.

A Pictorial Representation of the Soul

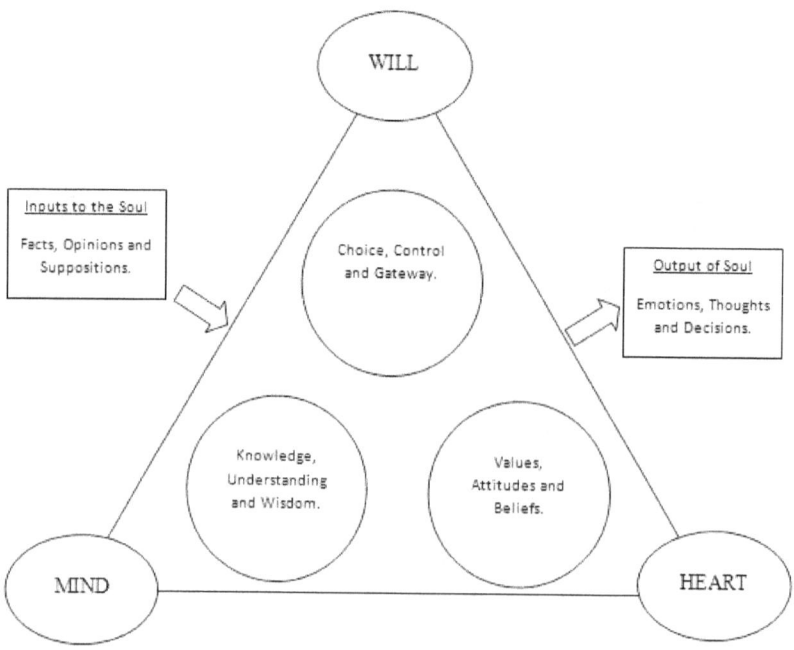

EMOTIONAL PRISONS

PART 2

THE DEVELOPMENT

Emotional prisons are not something that appear when we become adults. They can often be originated when we are in the womb or when we are very young.

In this section we look at two very important events in the life of a human that lead to lifetime problems; abandonment and abuse. We also look at a method of analyzing a person's dysfunctions based on four identifiable emotionally based factors; Security, Performance, Acceptance and Responsibility.

We then take a quick glimpse at how these four factors impact a person during their years of leaving the family of origin; adolescence and early adulthood.

5

ABANDONMENT

The concentration camp is the final expression of human separateness and its ultimate consequence. It is organized abandonment.
Arthur Miller.

Now that we have looked at the characteristics of the Soul and its component parts, the Mind, Heart and Will, it is time to provide a little more color. What I am going to do in this chapter and the next two is to give you some examples of how the Soul works in the lives of children. I am going to show how each of its parts interacts to produce action. We are starting to get into the more practical side of this subject of "Emotional Prisons."

Before I get into some illustrations of how our Soul's parts work with each other, I want to qualify this chapter. I am going to show how things work, but remember my writing is also a product of how the parts of my Soul work together. I am as fallible as any other person. For this reason you may find that some of what I write you may not connect with, or you might just outright disagree with my interpretation of what I see. This is okay, and I expect it to happen. The whole point here is for all of us to see that the nine parts of every person's Soul function together at some level.

The beginning point for all understanding of how the Soul does things inside itself is to acknowledge that everything we know came in through the gateway of the Will. This is a very profound statement, and to fully grasp the implications of this will assist us in our perception of how the Soul operates.

The Beginning

The starting moment is the instant of conception; this is the actual moment in time that God creates a new Soul. The Soul didn't exist until that very moment in time. In terms of human biology, the moment of conception results in a single cell, which we call a fertilized egg, or more properly, an embryo. This means that every human embryo contains a Soul. It is this truth that is the basis for the moral opposition to human embryonic stem cell research, and also for the anti-abortion movement. This truth is also the basis for acknowledging that Soul development begins from conception and not from a later date, such as the physical birth date.

A good question at this point is, "What does the Soul do, or experience, during this time of growth of its home, the body?" Let us think about it. In the womb the Soul experiences all kind of inputs into and through its gateway. It hears noises, feels movements and senses light. It tastes the fluid it is living in; it feels the walls of the womb, and sometimes kicks out as it uses its little muscles, experiencing its personal environment. All these things provide the Soul with input, and begin to build some form of knowledge database. The unborn baby learns the patterns of the mother, the resting, the getting up and moving, the heartbeat. It learns about exterior intermittent sounds, like music, or aircraft noise and dad's voice. It feels the warmth or cold of mom's exterior environment, it senses daylight. Sometimes the baby even sucks its thumb!

What is harder to figure out is how this impacts the new Heart. Does the baby have emotional responses to all this Soul input? I'm not any kind of expert on this, but I suspect it does. I'm thinking that the baby, even in the womb, has a sense of security and comfort, and it feels connection to its mother. It may even develop an appreciation for Dad, assuming he regularly talks to her or him. It wouldn't surprise me if some children were born with an incompletely developed understanding of their musical tastes. The biggest clue to me about this answer is that the baby seems to "know" mom and recognize her quickly after the birth. How could this happen without learning and connection?

Development

Much like a person's physical body, a Soul has to develop and grow. The big difference is that the physical body develops primarily because of the biochemical input of the parents, genetics. The genetic input of the two biological parents decides the general physical attributes of the new person they have conceived. After the birth, the environment and lifestyle of the child adds to, or changes, the genetically pre-programmed body.

The Soul is different; its growth is totally dependent on input from outside of itself. Consider the situation of any individual who is born into the American culture. They grow up as an American, speaking the American language, eating American food, playing American games, and so on. More importantly, they have American values, beliefs and attitudes, they

43

know facts from an American perspective, and they understand the American way. Now, what if we take that person and give them to a family of people from the Indian culture or Chinese culture? We all know that they would grow older physically looking pretty much the same in any culture; for example they would have the same skin color, the same height and the same eye color. We also know that they would develop a totally different set of values, attitudes and beliefs. Their Soul would develop differently!

Emotional Prisons – The Formative Years

It is in what we typically call, "the formative years" that we can be aimed at an emotional prison. The individuals having the responsibility for providing what we call care-giving are the people who provide these young Souls with their important and Soul-developing input. This group of care-givers are primarily parents, but also include extended family, neighbors, daycare workers and educators. The young Soul is immature, naive and very accepting. It takes in through its gateway almost everything it sees and hears, and accepts it as truth. As adults, we have learned that not everything the world offers us is true or healthy for our Souls. However, children are not able to recognize or comprehend this. Let us look at two of the things that our children might experience, abandonment or abuse (covered in the next two chapters), and relate this to how they may act later in life.

Abandonment

When we consider the term "abandonment" we think about things like the abandonment of newborn children by their mothers, or maybe a parent leaving the home, spouse and kids behind. To me these are certainly types of abandonment, but they really don't fully describe the subject well because they focus on a physical action only. My understanding of abandonment is more inclusive than that. I believe all abandonment is emotional abandonment.

We tend to think of abandonment as a leaving behind event, as is true of the two situations in the previous paragraph. The reality is that when someone is abandoned, the person doing the abandoning is making a choice out of his or her emotions, which I have previously called acting out. There are many examples of how young Souls are abandoned in our culture, and I want to go through some of them here.

When a distraught mother leaves her newborn baby somewhere she is acting out. We cannot determine the motivation easily, but we can be sure it is an emotionally driven decision. It could be because the mother wants the baby to be "taken care of"; she believes that she cannot do that adequately and that others might do a better job. As we have identified before, beliefs are a function of the Heart, so this is an emotionally-driven choice that is made by her Will. Maybe the mother doesn't want to take care of the baby and regards it as a burden. Abandonment here is again emotionally driven; the baby is not valued by the mother. How about the even worse situation, where the father forces the physical abandonment of the baby. It is his emotions and selfish desires generated in his Heart from his personal values, beliefs and attitudes that prompt this.

There is a case where a baby is given up voluntarily; we call it adoption. This is not abandonment; this is a rational, meaning a thought through and wise, choice made by the Will with input from the Mind and Heart. It is done primarily for the benefit of the child. I would agree that it is also an emotional situation, but it is not acting out. We have all heard of cases where adoptions have been forced on adolescents who have had children, by the biological grandparents of that child. Again, though, this is the grandparents usually trying to make a wise and rational choice for everybody involved.

Small Children - Big Damage

The most significant abandonment in our society, in terms of long term "Soul damage", occurs in the life of children after they have developed their own identity. Through the early part of life a child is totally dependent on the parents or other caregivers. From their perspective, they are part of the mother. They soon start to break free and move into a sort of interdependent phase, which is where they still receive significant attention and care, but feel free to experiment with their own choices. Then at about two years old they are more independent, and have begun to form their own identity. This is, of course, known as the terrible twos!

By this time, a child is mobile, can communicate and make his or her own interesting choices. The Soul has begun to take shape, the knowledge base has been building, understanding is developing and some wise choices have been made. In their vulnerable Heart, values, beliefs and attitudes have become apparent, and the Will demonstrates the ability to make controlled choices, with the gateway still being open to most things as they are into learning life's lessons. They don't know it but they are still dependent on their parents for their sense of well-being and personal value.

It is from this time on, and it lasts into the teenage years, that the child is most vulnerable to parental abandonment. I am going to reiterate here that all abandonment is emotional abandonment. Now let's go through a few examples of what I am talking about.

Parental separation, often resulting in divorce, is the single most obvious example of emotional abandonment. When a parent moves out, he or she breaks the physical and emotional connection with the child. It looks like only physical abandonment, but that is the adult's view. From the child's perspective, they have lost something, and their sense of well-being and importance to the adult is shaken deep into their fragile Soul. In their Heart, where they used to believe they were important to the parent, a new belief is formed, and that is "I am not valuable."

I do want to say here that in a parental separation situation, if the two parents can put aside their differences and place the needs of the children above all other needs, some of the bad effects of the separation can be mitigated. In fact, if this course of action is used, marriages and families can be saved. For a couple with children considering a divorce, a change of attitude, sometimes put as a change of Heart, can save the children significant long-term problems. I am speaking here from first-hand experience. I did not do this, and I ended up divorcing my first wife. I was totally selfish, and while I did think about the children, I did not make them my number one priority. There have been resulting problems, and I hope you forgive me for not divulging them out of respect for the other people involved.

I originally wasn't going to do this, but after what I expressed above about my own life, I want to put the issue of "divorce" into a godly frame of reference. In the last book of the Old Testament, Malachi 2:16, God says this.

"For I hate divorce," says the Lord, the God of Israel.

While I'm somewhat against speaking for God, I'm reasonably sure that one of the reasons He "hates" divorce is because of what it does to children. If you or any person you know is considering this action, please reconsider. It is a superior moral choice to do whatever we can for reconciliation than to break up. God does not forbid divorce, He strongly

46

advises against it. It is wise to seek counsel about how a divorce and the emotional abandonment of children will affect everybody involved in the long term.

The lost parent is another good example of abandonment. Consider a family where one or both of the parents is physically or psychologically absent (or both). There is a grave lack of emotional attachment between the young Soul and the parent. It could be due to work schedules, voluntary or involuntary, or may be due to some form of addiction like drugs, alcohol or pornography. Whatever it is, the result is the same, lack of emotional connection for the child with the parent. The internal "new belief" result for the child is the same, "I'm not valuable", and "things around me are not okay, therefore I'm not okay."

Neglect

My next example of abandonment is neglect. When we are not taking care of our kids in a consistent and appropriate way, we are not taking care of their needs. While our children may not completely realize that they are not being treated with adequate care, they do eventually start to connect the dots. Neglect can take two major forms, physical or psychological. Physical neglect can be as simple as not feeding the kids in appropriate ways, but can also include not caring for their hygiene or getting them exercise. Psychological neglect is worse in some ways, because the damage is not easily visible. It includes things like not teaching normal social skills, not giving caring hugs or some other form of affection, and not listening to them as they tell us about their life. If we are not valuing our own children, what are they going to think and feel inside their Soul? Yes, it is the same result, low self-worth; they can sense the lack of love in the lack of attention to needs.

I have come across many examples of neglect, though some of them are hard to identify as neglect and often get misinterpreted as something else. So here are a few of the actual examples I've seen first-hand.

- A child sits outside a bar while Dad pops in for a "quick one", but he doesn't come out for a long time.
- Mom goes into the store for a few things, leaving her two kids out in the hot car, even though the window is down, they still get overheated.
- Mom frequently forgets to pack lunch for her kindergartener.

- The laundry doesn't get done in time; the kids have to wear clothes that are already dirty.
- Parents don't allow their children to play with other children much, thereby denying them the opportunity to learn normal peer relational social skills.

Mostly, neglect occurs when one or more of the parents are attempting to get their own needs met. The problem is that it is at the expense of the children. The children pay because they develop inaccurate and negative internal concepts of their personal value.

Unavoidable Abandonment

Now I come to the last example. This is the hard one, because this happened to me! Sometimes abandonment happens outside the control of the parent. It could be due to a natural disaster, like the hurricanes that hit New Orleans in 2005, or a prolonged illness of a parent or child, or maybe even the death of a parent. Whatever the cause, the result is still the reality. Inside a child, who is desperately seeking an answer to "why is this happening", new false beliefs are formed. The little Soul is damaged. Things that were true one day are not true the next, for the child it is confusing and results in those two things. "I am not valuable" and "things around me are not okay", or put another way "I don't feel secure anymore."

As I said above, this happened to me! When I was three and a half I developed tuberculosis. The only treatment available at that time was a new drug regimen, and separation from the community, a form of quarantine. I was delivered to the sanitarium for treatment by my parents, and left there. I was abandoned! My mother has told me that she could hear my screams from outside the building. This added to her burden of guilt, as she knew she was abandoning me. This guilt, as I've tried to tell her, is false guilt, because she was actually saving my life! If my parents had not abandoned me, I would not be writing this book. There is much more to this story, which I will be discussing later where appropriate.

What Do Abandoned Kids Do?

The real question here is if a child is abandoned in any of the ways described above, what could we expect? To be able to answer this with some degree of logic we ought to look at what the life of the Soul is like for the child before abandonment and then look at under their new circumstances.

In our pre-abandoned child, the Soul is in full growth mode. The gateway is opened almost all the time; the child is receiving input from parents, other family members, educators and other worldly sources, such as TV, books and the Internet. Obviously, the older the child gets, the less influence a parent will have and the more weight the rest of the child's world will have. Information is coming into the Heart and Mind of the child through the gateway, and most of it sticks. Knowledge, values and beliefs are established inside the Soul, and then gradually understanding of what this knowledge means and how to use it develops. Attitudes are formed, and choices made, good and bad, with resultant behavior, or output from the Soul showing itself.

The Soul is working well, in the sense that the parts are functioning as designed. It is a little like a car that is driven by a novice who jumps on the gas pedal, and then on the brake, while they are constantly turning the steering wheel backwards and forwards. The car is working, but the driver has not mastered the art of driving. So our growing Soul makes some mistakes and some good decisions, and as it does this, it receives feedback. This feedback provides new information through the gateway, and knowledge, values and beliefs are refined and hopefully improved. This is called "growing up." Some of the important aspects of growing up are the building of self-confidence, the development of understanding of who we are, and the knowledge that we are secure. It is these three things that are attacked when a child is abandoned.

We've taken a glimpse of how the young Soul works in a typical family situation, now let's look at what happens when one parent leaves. There is new information taken in by the child through the gateway, and his or her immediate world has changed. The intimate contact with the parent who left is broken, or at best diminished. The whole basic frame of reference of the child has changed. Inside this developing Soul, new knowledge is placed in the Mind, and new beliefs are formed, based on these new facts. Turmoil and confusion are present in the little one's Heart. There is a chain of thinking that begins to develop, and it could be something like this.

I had two parents, now I have one. I used to be cared about by two people, mom and dad, but now there is only one person who cares. They don't care for me like I thought; I'm not worth caring about. I don't feel so secure, and when I'm anxious, I only have one person to call for, so I'm not sure I can cope with that any more. I don't understand what is going on, or if I'm important like I was. This hurts, I'm not sure what I am, and I'm not sure who I am. I don't feel good about my life right now; I don't feel good about myself.

Can you see how the Mind and Heart are communicating with each other, and beginning to come to a new type of understanding and belief about the "Who am I" question. A child in this situation can then move on into further sets of thinking and feeling patterns deep inside, without even showing this to the two parents. For example, they can begin to believe that they, the child, must take care of themselves, and any love they want or need has to come from inside. This could be the beginning of an insular, or narcissistic, child, who grows up to be a totally self-centered adult, who ends up in an emotional prison. This child may choose to draw themselves in and begin a lifetime of depression, and then begin to self-medicate with food, drugs or sex when they are older, another prisoner of emotions.

I hope you would agree that abandonment is a serious issue with many long-term repercussions. The effects of abandonment often get buried or go in a hibernating state and resurface later in life as some form of dysfunctional behavior. I believe that is why God said this about it in the book of Deuteronomy 31:6:

"Be strong and courageous, do not be afraid or tremble at them, for the Lord your God is the one who goes with you. He will not fail you or forsake you."

This is Moses speaking to all believers across the ages. He is giving us God's promise that He will never fail us or abandon (forsake) us. For me this means that no matter how rejected, lonely or disillusioned I am feeling, I know that God has personally promised me, based on my faith in Him, that He will always be there. If you have been abandoned, not just as a child, but at any time in your life, open the gateway to your Soul and take this promise as God's personal promise to you, into your Heart. This is a way you can believe God in your life and it will help deal with any lingering pain or hurt left inside you due to your abandonment experience.

Having covered the very important subject of abandonment, I want to now cover, in the next two chapters, an equally important issue affecting the Souls of our children, abuse.

6

CHILD ABUSE AND THE ABUSER

Child abuse casts a shadow the length of a lifetime.
Herbert Ward

In this chapter and the next we are going to take a look at the subject of child abuse, a topic we can respond to with the raising up strong emotions in all of us. The objective here will be to develop an understanding of what goes on inside the Soul of a person who abuses and how it affects the Soul of the victims. Almost every person has been touched by child abuse in some way, either directly or indirectly. I am no different. While I am not a victim of abuse, I have been a witness of it in the lives of people around me. I am now going to share a couple of those stories, and both have tragic endings for the perpetrator. The victims and their family members will, of course, never be rid of their pain. In some cases this pain can become the force that directs a person into an emotional prison, which we will discuss to a limited extent below, and in more depth later.

When I was growing up there was a single mum (in the UK we have Mums not Moms) who was raising two kids. They lived about one block from my home. One day there was a news item on TV about one of them who had killed himself. One of my neighbors had committed suicide; he was only seventeen. It was speculated on why he had done this, and at age eleven it was a very surreal experience for me. Over the weeks that followed we discovered that he had been abusing young boys in the area, but not near where we lived. He had hidden this activity, but had eventually been exposed by one of his victims. He chose to end his life instead of facing the consequences; he was the final victim of his own actions.

A few years ago a local high school coach walked in front of an eighteen wheeler on a local freeway, and got hit and killed. The rumors flew; marital trouble, financial problems and manic depression. Upon investigation, the authorities discovered a history of sexual encounters with high school girls. He also became his own final victim!

Abuse

When we say this word "abuse" in the context of the lives of our children, we all conjure up a mental image of what we think it means. For our purposes I am going to use the very simple description given in Webster's dictionary, which says:

"Abuse is – to injure by maltreatment."

This subject, abuse, means so many different things to people that it is somewhat hard to find a common ground for discussion. I've come to develop an understanding of it from talking, but mostly listening, to so many individuals who have been on the wrong end of abuse. What is also enlightening is that I've been able to hear what perpetrators of abuse say about their actions. Crystallizing my understanding down to something generic about abuse I would say this. Abuse is acting out.

As we have discussed before acting out is short for acting out of one's emotions. So that when I say the abuse is acting out I am clearly identifying that abuse has an emotional origin within the perpetrator. Please note, I am saying nothing here about the innocent victims of abuse; that subject will be covered in the next chapter.

Maltreatment to the point of injury of children, which is abuse, comes in many forms, and we use many adjectives to qualify what we may observe as we narrow down the focus of a situation. Example adjectives that are typically utilized with the word "abuse" are physical, sexual, emotional, mental, verbal, psychological, spiritual and sometimes neglectful. On the face of it, by looking at this list, there seem to be two broad categories of abuse, physical and psychological. However, let us consider abuse from a results perspective.

While abuse can have a physical expression, as in a beating or incest, it always has a psychological aspect. The reverse is not true. For example, emotional abuse doesn't have to involve any kind of physical aspect. In fact, it is entirely possible to abuse someone who is on the other side of the world, using the phone or the internet. This leads me to say that all abuse is psychological in nature, whether we consider it from a perpetrator or victim perspective. As a reminder, the word "psychological" means "of the Soul", having its origins in the Greek language where "psuche" (psyche) can be understood as "Soul" in English. Abuse is a Soul issue, and that makes it an emotional prison issue too!

For those of us that like one-liners for remembering important things, here's one on this topic. "Child abuse occurs when an immature Soul is injured through maltreatment by a more mature Soul."

Perpetrators

When you watch or read a story about an adult, or even an adolescent, abusing a young child, do you wonder, "What is it inside them that causes them to do such a horrible thing?" I do; in fact part of me thinks that a child abuser ought to be given the harshest possible penalty available under law. This is because I understand child abuse as Soul on Soul crime that has long lasting effects. The problem for me is, I know that these abusers are in their own kind of emotional trouble, an emotional prison. I, therefore, have to temper my desire to stop, then punish, abuse and abusers with an understanding that compassion toward the bad guy or gal is appropriate too.

Much has been postulated, written about and theorized on the subject of what drives a child abuser. Sometimes I get the sense that the experts in this subject are trying to find excuses for this kind of unacceptable behavior. The reality is that this kind of person, one who abuses an innocent child, is "Soul sick" and in some cases depraved. Even one instance of child abuse demonstrates that the perpetrator has a Soul that is not functioning well.

Our social and legal system is designed to protect the innocent and be compassionate to the criminal. I'll talk about the child victims in the next chapter, but the people who do these things don't seem to be adequately dealt with and often are repeat offenders. I think that while most experts in this field have a good understanding of the behaviors and psychological issues involved, they miss things too often. The thing they miss is just how deep the perpetrator's emotional prison is, and what they'll do to stay in their dysfunction.

The discussion so far leads me back to this major question. What is going on inside the person who does such things? Let us take a look at how the Soul of a child abuser might be operating. What is going on in there?

The straight up answer to this is "chaos." The Soul of an abuser is in complete disarray. It looks like he or she is out of control (self-control), but that is not necessarily true. We need to begin looking into the Soul of the child abuser by taking a moment to revisit the makeup of a normal Soul.

You probably recall that each Soul has three major completely interdependent parts, the Mind, Heart and Will. Each of these has their own three interdependent parts. The word picture we have used before is:

Mind – Knowledge, Understanding and Wisdom.
Heart – Values, Beliefs and Attitudes.
Will – Choice, Control and Gateway.

In a normal healthy adult these nine Soul functions would operate on an interdependent basis, which simply means that they would work together for the benefit of the individual. Inside the Soul of a child abuser something goes terribly wrong!

I want to take a short sidetrack here. Not every culture has the same approach or judgment about what constitutes child abuse. For example, some people believe spanking a child is wrong and is abuse. While others believe that spanking is acceptable unless it physically injures a child. Some even think it is okay to spank or beat a child into submission. The point here is that each culture has their own perspective on what the acceptable treatment of children is.

Most societies have laws which govern the issue and that lay out these acceptable boundaries for the people to follow. Also, in most cultures there would be some unwritten rules regarding the right and wrong of actions toward children. An example of an unwritten rule could be that spanking should be done in private. Whether codified or not, the child abuser has grown up with these laws and rules, and is to be held accountable to them. Let us go back to looking inside the Soul of the child abuser.

Inside the Will of an abuser

Beginning at the end, which is the action of abuse, we can very obviously state that a child abuser has made some bad choices, but is that really true? This is a tricky question. For most people, the action of harming a child is definitely wrong, but for the abuser, it may look different though. An abuser can very easily view the choice to harm a child as acceptable, just like you or I find it acceptable to watch an R-rated movie, when others might not. For the abuser, the choice to abuse can be just a normal everyday decision.

Inside the Will of a child abuser, he or she chooses to abuse, and this is done under total self-control, allowing their choice of action out through the gateway. The actual action of abuse from only the perspective of the Will seems somewhat rational. Of course this is nonsense because we can't look at things in this way, we have to consider the whole activity of the Soul, due to its interdependent nature. My purpose in looking at this from only a Will point of view is to demonstrate that something else is going on other than a bad choice or out of control behavior.

The child abuser's Will is fed input from the Mind and Heart prior to making that choice to abuse. So to find an answer to our question about what makes someone do such a thing?" we must look at some of the thinking and feeling that is occurring inside an abuser. Let's start with the Mind.

What is happening in the Mind of an abuser?

The Mind of an abuser is a difficult thing to figure out. We know that the Mind is the center of knowledge, understanding and wisdom inside the Soul. There is also a sort of obvious characteristic that comes into play in our analysis. It is the sterile nature of a Mind that I'm thinking of. The Mind has no values, beliefs or attitudes associated with it; these things are a part of the Heart. The Mind has to connect and work with the Heart to obtain any moral or ethical input. The Mind can be "cold" when it is operating on its own. This is what is going on inside the Mind of the child abuser; it is cold and is not connecting adequately with the Heart.

A child abuser has, by the time they begin to abuse, acquired their own dysfunctional knowledge, understanding and wisdom. While it is true that we cannot read another person's Mind, we can through observation and analysis, make some reasonable inferences about what is going on inside it. The child abuser has a very conflicted situation in his or her intellect. Let's take a look at it.

First, they know certain things, meaning that they have a knowledge of matters which they consider facts. Using the example of spanking, they might know, for example, that their culture doesn't allow spanking. They also might know that their family always spanks the kids whenever it seems right. Even in this simple example we can see that these two knowledge facts conflict with each other.

Second, an abuser understands the potential consequences of his or her actions. Using our spanking example again we can see that if an individual spanks a child, he or she can expect consequences. In Chapter Two we recognized that understanding can also be called discernment, and the child abuser can be very discerning from their own perspective! By this I mean that the person who spanks might discern that if the spanking occurs in a grocery store it is very public and they might be reported. But if they wait until they get to their vehicle, they will be able to do it with impunity. Worse (maybe) than that, if they wait until they reach home the spanking can be a really "good" one. The child abuser in this example is conflicted in that there is no single understanding of how to conduct a spanking.

Third, the child abuser develops wisdom about how to conduct the abuse. They know right and wrong, from both their own and society's point of view, they understand the potential consequences of their range of choices, and now they apply these two in their own wisdom. Getting back to the spanking in the store situation, our child abuser might interact with the Will to select a course of action. Wisdom might tell the potential abuser to look around, and if nobody is in the aisle at the store, pop the kid one! It might also say, wait until we get to the car, you can do it there, while the child still remembers what he or she did. Or wisdom might say wait until we get the child home, because you can use the belt then. Again, there is that same conflict.

Putting this all together we can pick up that the Mind of an abuser will probably always have some form of conflict going on. I want us all to notice that I haven't said "confused" in describing the state of the abuser's Mind; this is deliberate. The abuser's Mind is not confused; it is cold and calculating, assessing every situation that might involve the ability to abuse the young person. To me, the reality is that an abuser is so cold to their abusive nature that they think only of what the act of abuse does for them. The damage that an abuser is doing to that young Soul is of no concern or importance.

I have used the very innocuous example of spanking here, so I want to spend a moment or two looking at more egregious abuse. One of the worst, from a long-term consequence perspective, is sexual abuse of a child. It doesn't really stretch our Minds to understand that any level of sexual abuse toward a child, from the perpetrator's view, is all about them.

To be able to sexually abuse a child, the abuser has to have rationalized the action in their Mind as acceptable. This statement is true of all child abuse; the Mind has rationalized it as **acceptable**. And this is because the abuser has lost his or her moral compass, which is found in the Heart.

The Heart Fails

We have looked at the Will and Mind of the child abuser and have made a sort of obvious claim, that they are not working well, and they are not operating in an interdependent way. And so it is with the Heart; it too is operating without real or adequate connection with the Mind and Will. I am reminded of a couple of Scriptures when I think about this.

The first is from Proverbs 4:23:

Watch over your Heart with all diligence, for from it flow the springs of life.

The next is from Jeremiah 17:9:

The Heart is more deceitful than all else and is desperately sick; who can understand it?

The first verse tells us that it is from the Heart that "the springs of life flow." This is very simple and profound at the same time. It informs us that our very nature, our character, and our actions all flow out of our Heart. The second verse is a warning from God, explaining to us that our Hearts can deceive us. (As an aside, this is the core reason that God says we are to give Him our Hearts, so He can help us overcome this "sickness" inside it.) With an abuser of any kind, the Heart has become so sick that it totally misleads the whole Soul, resulting ultimately in sick actions.

Earlier in the chapter I had stated that the Soul of an abuser is in chaos, and now we are coming to the reason this is true. The Heart of an abuser is so sick that it cannot provide the Soul with any real moral guidance. In this sense I am talking about both socially acceptable and spiritually acceptable behavioral direction.

You probably recall that the Heart is where a Soul's values, beliefs and attitudes reside. Since we know what a child abuser does, we can make a shrewd assessment of what his or her values, beliefs and attitudes are. I want to take a look at some of these things.

57

For one human being to inflict abuse on another takes a deep-rooted belief that it is okay to do it. For example, if a father sexually molests his daughter, somewhere in his Heart he believes that this is acceptable. That just boggles my mind! I cannot connect with that truth, but it is true; he really believes it is okay. This father values his need for sexual power or a sexual outlet over his daughter's need to be safe and secure. He has a mind-set or attitude that allows him to believe he can violate his own little girl and not have a significant consequence. Indeed he may even believe he can get away with it. As you read this, doesn't that thought disgust you?

The Heart of a child abuser is failing him or her; the sickness inside it has become so severe that nothing can stop it overcoming what the Mind and the Will may present as input. The emotions generated by the sick Heart overpowers them, and seek only their own satisfaction. Not only is the abuser's Soul sick, but also it is trapped in the emotional prison of self-gratification. I think of it as similar to being in a medical ward of a prison, a desperately bad situation. Not only is a prisoner locked away, having no freedom, but he or she is sick as well. Our emotional prisoner is locked away in his or her own emotional prison, and is emotionally sick as well. When an inmate who is medically sick needs treatment, the jail brings in an outsider, normally a medical doctor, to intervene. The emotional prisoner who is emotionally sick on top of their incarceration will also need outside intervention to be able to get well. The child abuser may have to receive intervention from several sources, such as the police, child protection services and the courts, and this is because they are unable to help themselves.

Chaos in action

When you combine the weak Will, the cold Mind and the sick Heart, and then add the fact that they are not interacting well with each other, is it any surprise that dysfunctional things happen? It is Soul chaos, and when it is happening in the life of our children, it is a real life horror story called child abuse. We can all identify with the statement "they need help" when we talk about child abusers. I hope that now you might have a sense of just how much help they really do need.

The chaos inside an abuser's Soul wreaks havoc on the victim, which I am going to talk about in the following chapter. There is a Scripture that I think speaks to the issue, and I have never seen it used this way, but here goes. In the book of Colossians 3:21 God gives us a very important instruction:

Fathers, do not exasperate your children, so that they will not lose Heart.

This verse is set in a section of the Bible that speaks to the subject of family relationships. Although it uses the word "fathers", on occasion the original Greek word is translated as parents, which philosophically includes extended family members like grandparents or uncles, aunts and cousins. Unfortunately we also know that most child abuse occurs between a child and a family member. This means (to me) that this verse speaks to the abuser directly.

When we understand how the Soul of a person works, and more particularly the Soul of a younger person, the verse can start to take on a really strong meaning. Consider this verse in the knowledge that parents, or any significant adult in a child's life, can basically push almost anything through the gateway of child's Soul. In fact this is the way we reach our kids sometimes, by forcing a lesson from life into their Soul. What if we are an abuser, and choose to misuse this capability?

In the translation I used above it uses the word "exasperate"; some other translations say it as "provoke to anger." When an adult forces something through the gateway of a child, they run the risk of "provoking" the child. Think of it as taking a finger and directly prodding the actual physical Heart of the child. To do this you would have to invade the body of the child, which is of course okay for you, but dangerous for the child. So it is with the Soul. When an adult forces themselves on a child, it is risky for them. When an abuser forces themselves on children, it always harms the Soul of a child.

So, in the context of our discussion here, I am going to paraphrase the verse like this:

Adults, don't reach into a child's Soul by invading it with your own stuff, you will stimulate the child to lose their sense of healthy boundaries, to develop internal anger and to become fearful of others.

This paraphrase brings us to the point where we can look at the results of child abuse in the Souls and therefore lives of our children.

7

THE ABUSED CHILD

The sexual abuse and exploitation of children is one of the most vicious crimes conceivable, a violation of mankind's most basic duty to protect the innocent.
James T. Walsh

In this second part of the two chapters on child abuse we are going to discuss the effects of an accountable person (adult or possibly even an adolescent) abusing a child. As in the first part of these two chapters, we are going to look at abuse as always being psychological in nature, and sometimes having a physical component. We have previously described this as a Soul-on-Soul crime. This reminds us that there is a perpetrator and a victim. In every case of child abuse the perpetrator exercises his or her power, and the victim is generally helpless and cannot resist.

Years ago, in a life issues class at a church I attended (probably better called a recovery class) there was a young lady in her late twenties called Karen. Over a period of months we all got to know her well! At least we learned her story, and all the women warned their husbands away from her. This was because the young lady had almost no boundaries, and a couple of single men found that out the hard way!

Her father had sexually abused Karen over a period of years into her mid teens. She had then, by her own declaration, really got into boys, meaning that she became promiscuous. After many failed relationships, and a wild college life, she had finally gotten married. It didn't last long, less than two years, because she was constantly seeking personal fulfillment outside of the marriage. After much counseling, she came to understand much of what happened in her life due to her behaviors was a result of the long-term abuse by her father. Even in her late twenties she struggled with "looking for love in all the wrong places." I don't know what happened to Karen, as she left the church without really saying goodbye.

I never forgot that lesson - the lesson of being understanding to people who act out in such dangerous ways, of not judging another person until you know the story, and of how violated a child's Soul can become. Karen's

60

father had damaged her, possibly for the rest of her life, and aimed her at her own deep and dark emotional prison of sexual bondage.

The Journey Begins

Karen's story probably begins in a very normal place, the arms of adoring parents. I know there are exceptions to this, but I doubt there are many, and that is because most children are welcomed into the world. Some parents may be concerned about the economic and physical burdens a child brings, but they rarely simply don't want the new child. Generally, there is not a plan to "dump the kid and run" or to injure the child in any other way, and certainly any thought about aiming a child at their own emotional prison is not present. But these things do happen, and we are going to look at the damage it does to these children.

Two chapters ago we looked at how the Soul of a child develops. We identified the time period from conception to somewhere around the early teen years as the "formative stage." This is when abuse of children puts them in a high probability of ending up in an emotional prison.

Is it possible to abuse a child that is not even born? Yes it is! Consider an unborn child that goes through a botched abortion, but lives. Has that child been abused? Why of course! How about when the father beats the pregnant mother? Both the mother and probably the child are being injured, abuse is occurring. Consider also if either of the parents is raging, perhaps with a lot of loud shouting. Or maybe, the mother is drinking or on drugs. So many bad things can happen.

Any or all of these bad things provide input to the Soul of the unborn child who cannot protect itself from such invasive behavior. There is no understanding of what it all means; it is like feeding a computer virus into the memory of a computer, it just sits there until it is activated.

Then comes the period right after the birth, when the child is totally dependent on the parents, completely helpless, and completely accepting. At this stage the child is like a Soul sponge, it will absorb input through all its physical senses into its Soul and accept it all as normal. When abuse occurs here, the child can only respond to the physical pain, but feels both Soul pain and bodily hurts. I don't know if I've ever seen anything that addresses the Soul pain aspect of very early child abuse, but that doesn't mean it is not happening.

Once a child gets into its first and second year we can begin to see that the child is starting to show their own personality and character. If abuse is occurring here there is the beginning of some response in the Soul of child. Although it is hard for a child to recognize that what they are experiencing is what an adult might call abuse, they do have a sense that it is not right.

When my eldest was still very young, I think about a year and a half old, I remember an incident. My ex-wife was having one of her raging outbursts. I have no memory of what it was all about, but I remember my daughter's reaction. We both looked at each other, my daughter and I, and she shrugged her shoulders, as if to say, "What is this all about?" It was a magical and comical moment, but of course it made the moment tenser, as the raging got temporarily worse. The point here is that children know something is not right, and they just can't figure it out.

Abuse in the Developmental Years

After the first couple of years of life things get much more serious for children. They have finally realized, at a low level of psychological awareness, that they are an individual, and have their own needs and desires. In a previous chapter we covered the subject of development, in which I said (Chapter 5 – Abandonment):

In their vulnerable Heart, values, beliefs and attitudes have become apparent, and the Will demonstrates the ability to make controlled choices, with the gateway still being open to most things as they are into learning life's lessons. They don't know it but they are still dependent on their parents for their sense of well-being and personal value.

It is this dependency that causes their immature Soul to continue to have an open gateway to whatever their parents, or other significant people, want to pour into them. Abuse, which is injury by maltreatment, is for the child, another input, like a TV program or the hearing of a story. It is accepted as something they must legitimately experience.

As the young Soul develops there is a constant interchange between the Mind and Heart. I like to think of it as the beginning of a long life of trial and error, that time tested and scientific method! We have all been through it; this is where we try or experience something and see how it turns out. Young children are doing this about almost everything, as they haven't built up a storehouse of knowledge, understanding and wisdom in their

Mind. Nor have they formed solid values, beliefs or attitudes in their Heart.

Imagine, if you can, what happens inside an immature child during an abusive episode. Let me use the example of a male child who is hit by the slapping of his father's hand so hard that it leaves a bruise. Inside the Soul there can be many responses, which will be mostly a function of maturity and prior experiences. I'm just going to go through one simple possibility.

The child experiences the slapping and immediate physical pain, and inside the Soul there exists a state of shock and confusion. Somewhere in his Mind the boy says, "This is the same father who talks to me, plays with me and touches me gently with his hand." Now he is shouting at me, and I don't understand, he is using his hand to hurt me, is he playing with me? The Heart is comparing the belief that Daddy is a safe person and wouldn't hurt me; with the reality that Daddy did hurt me. Daddy is important to me; I value him, why is this happening?

We can see from this abbreviated look at what might happen in the Soul of a younger abused child how thoroughly disorientating abuse is to him or her. From the perspective of long-term emotional damage, and emotional prisons, we can now begin to get a glimmer of what the outcome of abuse might be. I want to take a look at some of the more common outcomes.

Common Outcomes of Abuse in Children

The Trust Syndrome

First is what I call the "Trust Syndrome." I know a lot of people who read this will identify with it at some level. One of the problems a victim faces is that someone who they absolutely trusted, has abused them. The immature response is very naturally the defensive one, which is that nobody is to be trusted. Adults may have learned that this is not a truism, but children can't do that. The Trust Syndrome then is simply that the short-term reaction of a child to abuse of not trusting people, becomes a long-term value, belief and attitude. It is applied to everybody, family, friends, authority figures, and so on. It gets in the way of developing and sustaining what most of us might call normal relationships.

From the perspective of this book, there are widespread implications. People who cannot trust are vulnerable to getting their needs met through mechanisms other than human relationships. Examples are; sexual needs met through pornography, acceptance needs met through co-dependence and significance needs being met through materialism. Each of these is an emotional prison, and we can be placed there through the "Trust Syndrome."

The Pain Filled Life

A second outcome is the "Pain Filled Life." This is where the emotional pain that accompanies abuse is never dealt with adequately. I'm sure that most trained therapists would agree that dealing with the pain that accompanies abuse needs to be addressed as early as possible. It is also true though, that it can be dealt with later in life, but it is much more difficult. What is this pain? It is the emotional pain that will be present in all abuse. Emotional pain is "feelings of suffering or distress."

When a person is physically hurt, they experience pain. Sometimes it is minor, and it is left to go away by itself. At other times it is more serious and treatment is sought. It is the same for emotional pain. Sometimes it is minor, and we get over it and move on. The more serious level of pain though requires help, but an abused child doesn't know this, so it is internalized. When they are repeatedly abused, internalized feelings of emotional pain become a "normal" set of feelings to the abuse victim.

There are several important far-reaching results of this. Some of them become observable in early life; others start to kick in later as a teenager or even wait until adulthood. Probably the single most common result is self-medication. This is sometimes identified as addiction. We can self-medicate with drugs, alcohol, gambling, pornography and many more things. These do actually work, for a while. Our pain is temporarily lessened, and we feel better. However, eventually we get to a different point, and this is where the addiction develops what I call "secondary pain." This adds to the original pain making the situation worse. And, of course, all addictions are emotional prisons!

I probably need to be sure and say something here. While addictions are a common result of child abuse, that doesn't mean that an addict is necessarily the victim of abuse. Addictions are a response to or a way of dealing with emotional pain. Emotional pain can have many other sources, such as broken homes, betrayal from a loved one or ridicule in our teenage years.

The second and more horrifying result is that of generational abuse. In a twisted way, handing out abuse to others after you've been a victim is just "right." The abused child, in their pain, wants to inflict abuse on others, including their own kids and sometimes animals. This is then an emotional prison that a whole family can fall into.

When an abused child eventually falls into this long-term hole of generational abuse, something must have gone very wrong inside the Soul. The abused child has somehow rationalized that abuse is acceptable, as long as it is kept within certain boundaries, usually the close family (which might include family pets). The child has also come to an understanding that the abuse needs to be kept as a family secret. Once the family secret is out, the survival of the family unit is threatened by others, such as the police or child protective services.

Therefore, the abused child who then starts abusing sets up a dysfunctional family system. This system is not designed for growth and nurturing of its members. It becomes a place of getting the abuser's (the original victim) needs met, and a place of survival of the unit itself. This is why we ought not to be surprised when we suddenly hear that one of our neighbors has gone off the deep end and killed the family, or has been picked up and thrown in jail. Think about this next time you hear on the news that something like this has happened. It could be the result of child abuse that occurred a generation ago.

The Doormat Condition

The third and last outcome I want to cover is "The Doormat Condition." This is just as it sounds. An abused child can become a person who lets everybody stomp all over them, rubbing off the dirt from their own life onto the child.

Picture the victim, a young child receiving abuse. He or she is being delivered a message by the abuser. It could be verbal or non-verbal; the message always contains this component. You, the child, don't have value. The child absorbs this and begins to apply their limited ability to process Soul messages. The Heart and Mind work to try to make sense of the mixed signals they are receiving through the gateway. Signals like, I love you and I hurt you, I protect you and I use you, or how about this, you are important but my needs are more important.

It is easy to appreciate how difficult it is for an immature Soul, the child, to come up with some dysfunctional conclusions that help them to understand what is happening to them. Eventually the child becomes comfortable with their role, a combination of scapegoat, psychological punching bag and people pleaser. I've called it the "Doormat Condition." The child just acquiesces to this role over a period of time, and then carries it over into later life.

We can all make some shrewd guesses as to the kind of person the "Doormat Condition" generates. They can be a co-dependent, somebody who lives to please others and is not happy unless others around them are happy. They can be a person that gives their all in every situation, even when it hurts them. They can be a severely depressed and maybe non-functional person who just keeps their feelings bottled up inside. Whatever or whoever they turn out to be, they will always just take it, absorbing whatever the world throws at them without fighting back. The problem is; that is "normal" to them.

From the discussion above about abuse in the developmental years we can see that abuse results in severe long-term damage. Now I know that is probably intuitive to most of us, but I hope that we can all look at this subject with more of a knowledgeable eye from now on. Earlier I talked about how it is possible to miss some of the deeper psychological damage, and this is because it can be somewhat hidden from plain sight. This makes it difficult for a parent or counselor to help or provide therapy to deal with the longer-term problems such as the "Trust Syndrome", "Pain Filled Life" and "The Doormat Condition."

Any young child who is abused can end up in some form of emotional prison. Some are fortunate to be able to overcome being a victim. Others don't show symptomatic behaviors until later; for example Post Traumatic Stress disorders often arise years after the events to which they are connected.

Abuse in Later Childhood

Child abuse typically begins before this time that I have called "Later Childhood." This statement implies that it might be continuing. I think this is probably true for the more invisible forms of abuse such as verbal and emotional abuse. For the more visible abuses such as beatings, it could well have stopped, as the outward signs are less easy to hide or cover up. Also the slightly older victims are more able to know that the abuse is wrong with the possibility that they will tell somebody outside the perpetrator's sphere of influence. This means that continued abuse could result in exposure for the abuser, so he or she would cease the abusive actions out of personal survival.

The invisible abuses are much more easily covered up and less risky to the perpetrator, so they can continue without much attention to what anybody else thinks. This just adds more pain to the child's life.

By this time, later childhood, the child has begun to separate how each person in their life is relating to them. Some, and probably most, of the significant older people around them don't do the things that the abuser does. So with some important relationships emotional pain is present, and with others it is not. The more developed the Soul becomes, the more obvious this is to the child.

In addition to this newly dawning reality for the abused child, there is the inevitable comparison with other families. Unless the child is completely locked away, he or she will interact with other kids. It could be at school, or the neighborhood, or maybe at church, but it is going to happen. The abused child will eventually find a peer, and maybe even an adult, to talk to, someone they feel safe around. The invisible abuse will ultimately find its way into the light of the truth.

There is a Scripture that addresses this point, and I think it is valuable to see what God might have the say about this. It is found in Ephesians 5:11-13.

Do not participate in the unfruitful deeds of darkness, but instead even expose them; for it is disgraceful even to speak of the things which are done by them in secret. But all things become visible when they are exposed by the light, for everything that becomes visible is light.

Here the author, under God's guidance, is saying the following things:

1. Don't do deeds of darkness; in this context, don't abuse children.
2. Deeds of darkness are unfruitful; abuse of children has no practical benefit.
3. Expose deeds of darkness; if somebody knows abuse of children is going on, tell the appropriate parties.
4. Don't speak of these secret things; don't tell others who don't need to know; that is gossip.

5. All deeds of darkness become known with light; search for the truth, the perpetrator and the victim will be better off.

Some of what has been written above is intuitively obvious. The point here is that when a child is the victim of abuse it is up to us adults to act, and act in appropriate ways. We must never ignore any signs, visible or otherwise, of injury by maltreatment. This is not to be limited to physical signs, but also psychological signs such as acting out. Doing nothing is not an option!

A Few Words on Sexual Abuse

Now I come to perhaps the worst form of abuse I can think of, sexual abuse. There are books, magazine articles and seminars galore on this subject, so I'm not going to go through material that you can find elsewhere. I'm going to talk about it in the context of how it puts a child into an emotional prison.

In the ministry I work in through my church, which is a "recovery" ministry, I get to listen to the stories of many people who have had difficult lives. While this topic applies to mostly women, it also applies to a considerable number of men. I am speaking from my own observation here; sexual abuse is a major factor in the lives of many people who have had troubled lives.

When I speak of troubled lives I am thinking about individuals who have become alcoholics, cocaine users, promiscuous, sex and love addicts, deeply depressed, multiply married, homosexuals, workaholics, the list can go on. What I have discovered is that at first I learn about the presenting problem, which is the behavioral issue that finally causes someone to seek help. Then after some time has elapsed, and as these individuals become more open in the place of safety we provide, I learn more. So often behind the drinking or use of pornography or other issue is a person who has been sexually abused.

When I sit and think about it, I do recognize that I run across it frequently because of what I am involved in. However, I think about all the people who don't seek help that have troubled lives. Then I think about people who have perhaps had some level of problems in their lives, but not to the point that they need a great deal of assistance to work through things. Then I think about the people who have simply got over it (Which is a term I don't like because I'm not sure anyone can actually do that.) and lead peaceful and normal lives. That is when I realize sexual abuse is probably more common than any of us will acknowledge.

For the reader who may not connect with this subject, let me list the types of sexual abuse that I have personally encountered through helping others.

1. Fathers, uncles and male neighbors having sexual intercourse with female children.
2. Mothers and female teachers having sexual intercourse with male children.
3. Adults, male and female, fondling female children.
4. Adults, male and female, fondling male children.
5. Fathers showing pornography to their sons.
6. Fathers speaking to their sons in graphic sexual language.
7. Youth pastors having sexual relations with boys under their care.
8. Grandfathers "playing" in sexual ways with their granddaughters.
9. Neighbor boys forcing younger boys to have oral sex with them.
10. Older boys taking their parents porn movies and showing them to their friends and younger siblings.

While every individual who is in an emotional prison has a different story, I am sometimes struck by how many of them have been a victim of sexual abuse. It seems to occur in the later childhood part of their life, from about five or six years old up to early adolescence, and sometimes into the early teen years. It seems to me that when a child has been victimized in this way, the offender has most likely directed the victim's life toward some kind of emotional prison.

What is it about sexual abuse of a child that is so much worse than other abuses such as beatings or verbal assaults? To be able to answer this question we have to dissect what is going on during this abusive period. There are a few things to remember here. First, sexual abuse, while often thought of as being physical in nature, is also sometimes only a psychological event with no physical component. In every case it is the Soul of a younger person that is invaded, making all sexual abuse have one thing in common. Sexual abuse is always a psychological issue, whether there are physical aspects or not. The second thing to remember is that sexual abuse is always wrong, no matter how someone tries to rationalize it. It is Soul on Soul crime!

Perhaps the most important issue to try to always remember when considering this subject is the total betrayal it represents. Sexual abuse has sometimes been called "the end of innocence", and I like that phrase. When a child is exposed to this kind of abuse they can no longer see the world the same way again. I want us to try to put ourselves in the place of that innocent Soul to try to understand what is happening during these times of abuse. For anybody reading this who has been abused in this way, you may want to consider not reading this next section, although it will not be written in too graphic language.

No matter how the sexual abuse begins, or to what severity it is taken, one detail has to be true; a relationship existed before the abuse began. If no relationship exists, then the sexual action is not abuse; it is only (and I don't mean to minimize this) a sexual crime. Some people will not agree with that statement, and that is fine. My perspective is one of differentiation between abuse, which may or may not be a crime under whatever laws are prevailing, and a horrid crime. The difference is relationship. In the context of sexual abuse, a crime is committed by someone who may or may not know you; abuse is always committed by someone who knows you.

That differentiation can be difficult to swallow, so let me expound a little. It is intuitive that if a complete stranger comes up to a child and commits some form of sexual act, it is a crime. The pedophile, however, always tries to establish a relationship with the object of his lust. This turns the crime into abuse because he or she tries to form a Soul-to-Soul link before committing an act. Abuse from a family member or other known person already has an in-place relationship at some level.

We have looked at abuse from a perpetrators perspective previously, so now we are going to look at from the point of view of the victim. As I said earlier, sexual abuse is a total betrayal of the victim. When God made people, He put in us a need for relationship with other humans. Without looking up the Scripture, it does say "it is not good for man to be alone." I am using a reasonably broad understanding here, when I say it means that all of us need relationship. When sexual abuse takes place, the relationship is violated. Yes, sometimes the physical body is violated too, but in all cases a betrayal occurs, a Soul betrayal.

What exactly happens? The answer lies in the understanding of what a relationship is. Between an immature Soul (child) and a significantly more mature Soul there is a connection. No matter what kind of relationship, such as family or neighbor, there is a connection. The immature Soul has a certain level of trust for the more mature person, and is therefore vulnerable to them. When that trust is violated, betrayal occurs!

Before any abuse is handed out, inside the Soul of the child, there is a peaceful situation. The child knows in their Mind that the person, who later ends up abusing, is safe, meaning that there is no sense of potential maltreatment inside the young Soul. Inside the Heart of the child, they believe that this person is okay and will not harm them; they value the relationship, and have an attitude of respect toward the more mature individual. In short, they are trusting. This young person is open to whatever the more mature Soul sends their way; their gateway is open.

If we think about it, one of the characteristics of an abusive situation, particularly an ongoing one, is that the perpetrator emphasizes that the whole thing is a secret. This plays on the fact that the immature Soul is relying on the relationship as being safe, and that they will let almost anything into their Soul. The secret then becomes part of the relationship dynamics. This may explain why sometimes it is years later when a victim finally connects with the truth that this sick individual wasn't loving them, they were abusing them. They allowed the abuse to happen, because they trusted the individual concerned, and thought they, the trusted person, wouldn't do anything to harm them. Years later they realize the truth.

Outcomes

The whole point of this book is to open up a dialogue on emotional prisons, and I can't think of a better example than the result of sexual abuse. When a person is sexually abused, they are targeted for an emotional prison. I think it is almost an impossibility to say what kind of prison a victim might end up in; we can say that it is almost certain that they will be in one. Let me give you some examples.

Obvious examples of emotional prisons are promiscuity or sexual repression. Without understanding what is happening a person can become overly sexually active in their teen years, or possibly later. This is a "looking for love in all the wrong places" kind of issue. The young Soul has learned the lie, because of the abuse, that love and sex are the same thing. They get into a cycle of being "loved" and being unsatisfied, but they persevere, because it is what they know. Whereas the sexually oriented activity was abuse during childhood, it now would best be called "misuse." This is where "Karen", who I discussed at the beginning of the chapter, found herself.

71

At some point they, the victims who have fallen into sexual promiscuity, may finally begin to slow down, because they are constantly being hurt and betrayed, but the problem is still there. On top of the original damage further Soul havoc occurs, as they have been misused in inappropriate ways, which piles more betrayal on what they have already experienced. It is possible that they have developed some form of sexual, romance or relationship addiction, all obvious emotional traps.

For the sexually repressed person, life with the opposite gender can become a trauma. Fear of relationships that might hurt as much as the abusive one is a constant undercurrent of life. Even when a truly caring person enters their life, the survivor of sexual abuse will hold back, fearing emotional pain. It is, of course, not about sex, but about the possible emotional pain that might be the result of the new relationship. The most difficult situation exists for the sexual abuse survivor who is not consciously aware of what happened to them when they were younger.

This inability to function in a healthy sexual relationship can lead to a myriad of problems. Examples are avoidance of physical contact with a spouse, getting a job that keeps one away from the marital bed, freezing up during sexual activity and experiencing psychosomatic pain as a result of normal sexual activity. In some cases the individual puts themselves into an emotional prison. Examples of a prison might be chemicals, like alcohol or prescription drugs, or perfectionism, as a way to control the fear surrounding sexual activity. As strange as it might seem, pornography could be the method, and emotional prison, of dealing with the emotional pain left behind by sexual abuse, and yet still have the victim's sexual needs satisfied.

Does The Bible Address This Child Sexual Abuse Issue?

The Bible does not specifically address the subject of child abuse in any way, so the short answer to the question is "no." There are a couple of verses to look at which might help us to understand how God might feel about this issue. The first is a direct quote from Jesus out of the book of Luke, chapter 17:1-2.

He said to His disciples, "It is inevitable that stumbling blocks come, but woe to him through whom they come! It would be better for him if a millstone were hung around his neck and he were thrown into the sea, than that he would cause one of these little ones to stumble."

I think most of us would agree that child abuse of any kind could be called "causing one of the little ones to stumble." Jesus in this quote quite clearly demonstrates His characterization of the abuser when He talks about "Woe to him." This is a generic "him"; in the sense that it could be a "him" or a "her", but it is obvious that Jesus views the person as self-condemned by their own sinful actions.

The second piece of Scripture to consider here is the seventh commandment found in Exodus 20:14:

You shall not commit adultery.

Here, God, in His "Ten Commandments", instructed the whole of humanity to refrain from adultery, and he wasn't just talking about being true to marriage. This is God at His most compassionate. He knows that He created sex to be an intimate physical expression of love between one man and one woman. He also knows that we, as humans, are prone to doing things that are not in our best interests. In this case it is experiencing sexual activity without the commitment of a marital relationship. So he makes it simple for us; don't commit adultery. He loves us so much that He doesn't want us to experience the downside of violating His original design.

Child sexual abuse breaks the seventh commandment. It breaks it for the perpetrator, and worse than that, it breaks it for the victim. For most cultures, child sexual abuse is a "crime among crimes", and this is true even if you don't believe in God, or know what the seventh commandment is!

If you are a survivor of childhood sexual abuse, and haven't yet been able to come to terms with it, I hope you will consider looking for help. As I said earlier, we were made for relationships, and some of these relationships are to help us heal from our wounds. It may now be time to seek help, to seek a relationship with a person of the **same gender** who will be there to guide you from living with emotional pain to living in emotional freedom. I recommend that a **Christian therapist** who specializes in this area be looked for. If you know you have been on the wrong end of sexual abuse, be assured that you may be in an emotional prison and not be aware of it. A psychological counselor can help you get out of the pit, and help you move into a freer life.

The Final Word

Child abuse is never acceptable. It is never to be swept under the rug. It is to always be reported to the appropriate authority. For me, as an observer, I think of it in a slightly different light. I think it should always be exposed.

I say this as a person who believes that child abuse results in a minimum of two people who are trapped in emotional prisons. Exposure of this behavior is one of the first steps in healing for both the perpetrator and victim. Keeping the whole thing secret results in this "deed of darkness" staying dark, with all the dark results. It results in all the parties involved staying in their own, emotional prison.

8

SPAR – A KEY TO UNDERSTANDING

I have striven not to laugh at human actions, not to weep at them, nor to
hate them, but to understand them.
Baruch (Benedict De) Spinoza

The last three chapters covered the two subjects of abandonment and abuse of children. These were identified as major factors in the early lives of kids that would very likely point them at an emotional prison that they would find themselves stuck in, sometime in their adult life. I now want to introduce additional major factors that tend to affect us more as we get older. The factors I am going to discuss are universal, and will touch every person in some way. In this chapter, I am going to discuss and explain these factors as they relate to how our Soul operates, and also how they relate to emotional prisons. In the next chapter, I will apply them to the adolescent through young adult stage of life. The chapter following that will look at the young adulthood to full adulthood stage.

Before I discuss what these additional major factors are, I want to illustrate a couple of them with a two short stories from my early adolescence.

When I was about 12 or maybe 13 years old, our class was having an English literature test. It was on Greek mythology and I didn't know the material. So, I cheated. The problem was, I was exposed right in the middle of my bad behavior, during the test, in front of everybody. I got sent to the headmaster's office (in the UK where I grew up, the headmaster was what we call here, the principal). I sat outside that room for what seemed like hours, which was a real ordeal for me. I eventually got summoned, and was forced to explain myself. One of the most interesting things was, he didn't punish me, and I never knew why.

It was something like two years after that I had another unsavory event caused by my own behavior. My friends and I had learned to steal by shoplifting. We had become quite proficient, or so we thought! As usual, I was dared to steal a certain item from a small store we used to frequent. And, as usual, I thought I could get away with it. Naturally, my time had come, and the storekeeper caught me. He demanded my name and address, which I gave him, not even thinking about lying. He said he was going to call my parents and tell them what I had done. However, he had a change of Heart, and it wasn't good! The police arrived at my house about two hours later, and I hid in a closet trying to get away, I was very scared. I got a really heavy talking to, and that was all the punishment I received. That episode ended my shoplifting career!

What was it about these two stories that is so interesting? It is what the underlying motivations were; they were performance and acceptance. This gets me to the place where I can now introduce the four new major factors that help to push individuals into emotional prisons. They are:

1. Personal Security
2. Personal Performance
3. Personal Acceptance
4. Personal Responsibility

I call this, the "**SPAR**" factors (Security, Performance, Acceptance, Responsibility). These factors are always at work in our lives, and they cause us to mature or grow. Sometimes we move backwards, which likely is manifested in getting emotionally trapped. It is like when a boxer is sparring with an opponent. At times he or she is on offense and sometimes on defense, then once in a while the boxer is just bouncing around the ring. Rarely, if ever is the boxer standing still.

What is so important about these SPAR factors? How do they influence how we conduct our lives, and lead some of us into emotional prisons? I want us take a look, but before we do, we have to address a truly significant question that has not been looked at yet.

Where do feelings come from?

There was a time when I would have said, 'Stupid question, it is from the Heart!" That is the response that most of us would give, and most of us are completely wrong.

In the earlier chapter discussing the Heart, I called it the center of feeling, which could also be interpreted as center of emotions. That is true, however we must understand that term, "center of emotions", correctly. This does not mean that all someone's emotions are sitting there in the Heart, just waiting to be let out. It doesn't mean that we have an inventory of emotions sitting on the shelf waiting to be picked up. There is no "emotional supermarket" with Anger on aisle one, Frustration on aisle two and Jealousy on aisle fifteen.

It does mean that our emotions depend on what is on aisle one, two and fifteen. As it says in the "Heart" chapter, it is our values, beliefs and attitudes that actually reside in the Heart. Our feelings therefore depend on our values, beliefs and attitudes in some way; they are linked to these three Heart characteristics. So let me repeat the question, where do feelings come from?

The answer is this. When three things come together an emotion can be produced. First, a situation is present. It could be that an event has occurred, or it might be that we are meditating about a subject. Then we apply our Mind, meaning knowledge, understanding and wisdom, and also our Heart, meaning our values, beliefs and attitudes. Mix them all together, and we have a response, which we call an emotion!

You may recall that in the 'Heart" chapter we talked about acting out. We identified this as acting out of our emotions. Now we can put it together a little more. When we have a situation and apply the characteristics of our Mind and our Heart, we get a response inside our Soul that is called an emotion, and we act on this emotion. When an emotion is generated inside our Soul, we either let it out through the gateway of our Will, or we close the gate and keep it in. Some people refer to this keeping in as stuffing our emotions.

It is really that simple! Our emotions are generated this way, and because of this they are mostly temporary. While our Mind and Heart characteristics are generally, in the short term, the same day by day, the situation we are in changes. (As an important aside, I want to add that over longer periods of time the characteristics of our Mind and Heart do change in the sense that they mature and develop.) For example, if we are talking to someone and they say something that offends us, we might become hurt. Then fifteen minutes later we are in a new situation, and we have moved on past being hurt. This is the normal routine of any person's life.

Of course, sometimes we dwell on a situation and the emotion doesn't pass, but this is mostly the exception. What can happen is that we spend a great deal of time on situations and the associated emotions can consume us, maybe even for days on end. Being consumed by our emotions can lead to longer term Soul responses like developing grudges, deep animosities, or perhaps depression. Some of these internal reactions of ours can also contribute to us putting our Soul into an emotional prison.

Let me give you a practical example of this "emotion generation" in action. First consider a simple situation. Two people see a man beating a dog. The first person sees this and is horrified; they are a dog lover, and have values, beliefs and attitudes that say to treat dogs in loving ways. They go from being horrified to getting angry, because they know and understand (Mind characteristics) that dogs are man's best friend.

The second person is in a different position. They see the same thing, but they know that the dog beater has children who had been previously attacked by this very dog. The second person feels a sense of gladness. Their values, beliefs and attitudes about protecting children added to their knowledge of previous events causes a different emotional response than the first person.

Do you see how two people seeing the same event have two totally different, but equally valid, emotional responses? Although this is a simple example, it clearly demonstrates how an emotion is generated as I have described above.

Having taken this small but important digression I want to rejoin the SPAR discussion.

Personal Security

Have you ever heard somebody say something like, "He is so insecure!" or maybe, "She takes things so personally, she is so insecure!" Most of us have, and we have all developed at least a crude understanding of what being secure might mean. The essence of this issue is how each of us answers the following question:

How do I feel about myself?

As you read that question, how are you answering that? How do you feel about yourself? Most people would probably give an answer, "I feel good about myself." Others of us readily admit that the actual answer to the big question is, "I don't have a clue." Some of us might even say something like, "I feel worthless."

There are many responses that I hear to this type of question. The answer that all of us will come up with depends on three things; what is going on around us (our situation), what we know about ourselves, and what values, beliefs and attitudes we carry in our Heart about ourselves. Do you notice that this is the same three parameters that I described above when talking about where emotions come from?

Earlier we mentioned the phrase "He/she is so insecure." This was in the context of us looking at how someone had been acting. We instinctively knew that the person we were observing was telling us something about their internal Soul condition. What was it, what was being said, but in an unspoken way?

Trying to answer this requires us to look at the insecurity of a person as a dynamic, or constantly changing, condition. Think about it in the context of your own life. At times you have felt insecure about yourself, and at other times you have felt more secure. As the years have gone by there are probably less times of insecurity, with more periods of being reasonably certain that you feel okay about yourself. Even from one day to the next all of us can have moments of feeling insecure. Throughout our life the sense of how we feel about ourselves will constantly change, and it is important to understand why this is, and how it happens.

Personal security, or the lack of it, is impacted as we have noted before, by three things; the situation, the Mind and the Heart. In the world of science that is called a, "three variable problem." (A three variable problem occurs when there are three factors, each being variable in their own right, that influence an outcome.) It is going to help our understanding of personal security to look at the three variable problem in a somewhat scientific way.

Let us start by keeping the first variable, the situation, constant, and allow the other two to change. This means that the Mind and the Heart part of the analysis are going to be allowed to change so that we can begin to see what happens to our internal security level. Consider the example of being called a name; let's say that a good friend calls you an idiot.

When we are an adolescent, having a less developed Mind and Heart, this name-calling will impact us in some way. We would instantaneously match the name against what we know and understand about ourselves in our Mind. We would also instantly compare this understanding against what we believe about ourselves in our Heart. An emotion would be the result. None of us can say what that emotion might be, but we can make guesses as to some possibilities. At that age I might guess that if a best friend says that I'm an idiot that I would feel some shame or guilt. Whatever the emotional response is, I'm very likely to internalize it as a sense of insecurity.

Now consider the same message delivered to an adult, let's assume it is a forty-year old man. He will go through the same process as the adolescent, but his emotional response will be different. He may choose to completely dismiss the comment, only feeling some mild amusement. Or he might feel disappointed that his best friend had resorted to name-calling. Whatever the feeling might be, this forty-year old is less likely to end up having a moment of insecurity.

In truth, it is impossible to know how any person is going to emotionally respond to being called a name. We can say though, that it is generally true that as we become more mature, we will respond with increasingly less sensitivity to this situation, and with more personal security. This is because our Mind (knowledge, understanding and wisdom) and our Heart (values, beliefs and attitudes), have developed through learning and experiences to be able to process name-calling in a better way.

This methodology of looking at a static situation, but changing how the Mind and Heart approach it, can be used in any circumstance. I know that the following statement might seem obvious but I want to say it anyway. This is the reason that older adults, again generally speaking, deal with situations better. They tend to be calmer and more secure about themselves.

Now let us go one more step deeper into the analysis. We can use the same situation, name-calling, and this time we will assume that the Mind is also static. I know that this is almost impossible, that our knowledge, understanding and wisdom would remain at a fixed point, but please bear with me. This allows only the Heart (values, beliefs and attitudes) to actually be a variable factor.

Will our emotional response to the name-calling be constant? No, of course not! If we apply the values, beliefs and attitudes we might have at sixteen we get certain emotional responses. Then if we fast forward, with the same individual having the same mindset, but now at forty, we will get a different emotional response to name-calling. This is due to the fact that living life has added to or changed our values, beliefs and attitudes.

Now let us apply this analysis to keeping the situation static, name-calling, but keeping the Heart (values, beliefs and attitudes) at a fixed point. Our sixteen year old will respond emotionally in some way. When the sixteen year old is forty, and applies the same values, beliefs and attitudes, but a different mindset, we would get a different emotional response. At forty we know and understand more about who we are and how the world works, and we can apply our accumulated wisdom to this name-calling in improved ways.

What is the point of all this? Why have I put you through this very dry look at name-calling? It is to try to firmly place in your mind that how a person feels about himself or herself, how secure they are, is totally dependent on their Mind and Heart and how they interact with each other. This next statement, I'm sure, is intuitively true to all of us, but it has tremendous implications. It means that we all have some measure of control over how we feel about ourselves! We each have some power over if we feel secure about ourselves or not.

While each one of us doesn't have a lot of choice about what we allow into our Soul while we are young, that changes as we get older. When we are adults we can choose what we allow to impact us, and in this context, what might impact our personal security. We can choose whom we listen to, we can choose what we read, we can choose what to watch on TV, and most importantly we can choose to believe God or not.

Now it is time to move on to the second SPAR factor, "Personal Performance."

Personal Performance

Has this thought, or something like it, crossed your mind, "I'm glad I got that project finished, I feel really good about getting to the end of it." Or maybe you have thought or said something like, "I'm frustrated and angry, because I didn't get my house cleaned today." These are understandable and healthy emotional responses to our internal assessment of how successful we have been in our daily lives. They are also not how we actually feel! Let me explain.

I am going to rewrite the two statements in the way we normally respond to our own performance.

1. I'm glad I got that project finished, I feel really good about myself.

81

2. I'm frustrated and angry with myself; I failed to get my house cleaned.

Do you see the difference? In each example the person made the statement and related the feelings to him or herself. Most Christians can relate to this if I say it in this way. Don't confuse the sinner with the sin. You see, what we actually do in practice is to equate **what we do** with **who we are**. The question we ask of ourselves in the context of personal performance is:

How do I feel about myself, due to the things I do?

This is often the key unspoken question for someone who condemns him or herself. Someone who tends to feel better when they are performing well is under a great burden. They operate with a deep and abiding fear of failure, and they are on the proverbial "Hamster Wheel." Their problem is that their performance standard once reached, doesn't feel satisfactory in any way. So the bar is raised, creating a new cycle of stretching for good performance to find those good feelings again. What is happening inside the Soul of this person?

Consider a person taking a college entrance test. He or she knows that if they achieve certain test scores it will give them access to the colleges that they would like to go to. They believe that they have prepared adequately to be able to get to their desired test score level. So, before taking the test they feel confident about their ability to pass at the desired level. They take the test and do indeed get the necessary score. Everything went according to plan, all the hard work of preparation paid off, and they feel really good about themselves. Then it happens; somehow this idea gets introduced into their life, "**I could have done better.**"

They have just got onto the "Hamster Wheel!"

We all know what happens next. Our test taker starts to look at higher-level colleges; maybe they are beginning to think about Ivy League schools. More study follows, more testing takes place, maybe a better score is achieved. Perhaps sleepless nights follow, as the fear of not getting to the new standard begins to take hold. Stress, which is short for distress, becomes an ever-present fact of life, and that hamster wheel keeps on turning.

In this simple example we can see that at first, the situation of taking the test, combined with knowing what is necessary to pass and the beliefs and attitudes that the test taker has prepared properly, result in positive emotions for the test taker. They are confident before the test, comfortable during it and elated as they meet their goal. Life is good and they feel that they are King or Queen of the hill.

Then they get on the hamster wheel. The performance target has changed, and now they have a different situation. They also know how hard it is going to be to get to that higher test score. The new belief is that they actually aren't ready and prepared for this tougher challenge. So they hit the books, they study extra hours, ignore their social life and don't connect with their important relationships. Sounds like the beginning of workaholism doesn't it?

Eventually our test taker becomes confident again, and they take the test. A better score is achieved. The question now becomes, is it enough? If it is, the test-taker is elated again, which reinforces the "work to get good feelings" belief. Of course, this allows a whole new cycle to begin!

If the score is not sufficient, there is a problem. A new choice is then made. The college candidate might give up, get off the hamster wheel, and say he or she is satisfied with this, and move on. This choice is made when the person is not allowing the marginally lower performance than expected to determine their final emotional state. For others, this is devastating, they feel awful about themselves, and they just give up to hopelessness. A third response would be, that they feel disappointed and that they are a failure, so they get back on the hamster wheel. They are going to try again, searching for a better feeling about themselves.

I hope this college test score example has made the point about the link we seem to make between performance and feeling good. This approach can be applied to any everyday situation involving our actions. I am going to list a few examples, and I'm sure you can come up with some of your own:

1. A homemaker tries to keep a home pristine. This could be the beginning of the emotional prison of perfectionism.
2. A teenage boy tries out for the football team, but doesn't quite have what it takes, so he takes steroids. This is possibly the start of a chemical addiction, another emotional trap.
3. The executive reaching for the last percentage point of profit, works later and later. His stress levels increase so he starts to stop for a drink every night, to unwind. He is adding chemical dependency to his workaholism; both are emotional prisons.

4. New to college, an eighteen-year-old girl finds good grades are hard to achieve, she is used to better performance at high school. But when she hangs out with the boys she feels better, and slowly slips into a promiscuous lifestyle. Her emotional prison of sexual addiction has begun.

In my own life, this link between what I do and how I feel has played itself out. As I have said before, I was abandoned as a young child. Due to this, I started down the road of doing things well, performing, and it made me feel better about myself, even at the age of five. When I was eleven, I was required to take a special one-time exam, as all eleven-year-old English schoolchildren were at that time. If you passed you went to a special school, where only the top 11% got to go. I passed and that felt good to me at that time. I will say more about this event in the next section on acceptance.

I hope I've explained and demonstrated how this issue of equating what we do with how we feel about ourselves adequately. It is a major source of problems in our culture.

The preoccupation with performance can affect anybody. Now we come to the reason at the middle of this. The fear of failure! Once we have learned that doing things well is interpreted internally by our Soul in such a way that good emotions are generated we are set up for a problem.

The problem is simple to understand, failure is the opposite of success, and this means that failure will ultimately result in a lack of good feelings, or worse than that, bad feelings will be generated. When a person gets into this emotional trap, fear of failure becomes an ever-present truth. This fear can then result in their jumping onto the Hamster Wheel, and not only in our work situations, but also in everything they do.

We all know people who are driven by performance, and I am going to suggest that most of them have a fear of failure. When we live with someone like this, or work with him or her, they often transfer their emotional orientation onto us. If you don't share this need to perform, life with such an individual can be miserable. I know some of you reading this fully identify with this!

This paragraph is for all the "driven' people who may be reading this, commonly called Type A by the popular culture, and I am one of you. We can really drive the people in our lives, our spouses, our kids, and other significant individuals, kind of crazy. While I acknowledge that it can be difficult to back off doing things well, we don't have to demand perfection from those around us. I try to think of it like this, excellence is the objective, perfection is impossible.

Personal Acceptance

We have looked at how we feel about ourselves, and how we feel as a result of the things we do. These are internally generated feelings based on our perceptions of ourselves. Now it is time to discuss how others think and feel about us, and how we feel about ourselves as a result of that. These are feelings generated internally but based on our perceptions of external factors or situations.

We are now entering dangerous territory; none of us can read another person's Mind or Heart. There is no way that we can, under our own power, be sure about what another person feels toward us, about us or for us. The territory is made dangerous because of our attempts to answer this burning question.

How do I feel about myself, due to my perception of what others feel and think about me?

There is a core problem here, and this is central to understanding how damaging the answer to this question can be. The problem is one of power and control. When how we feel about ourselves is dependent on how we perceive others think or feel toward us or about us, we are effectively handing over control of our feelings to other people. This in turn will contribute to the decisions we make about our actions, or put another way, how we conduct our lives.

This is the very trap I fell into in the exam at age 11 example I gave earlier. I became a mini celebrity in my neighborhood, as I was the first person to achieve a passing grade. One of my friend's mothers even gave me some money. I felt good about myself because of what others said, felt and thought about me.

I want to go back to basics here, and discuss this in the context of how our Soul operates. As you may recall our Soul is made up of three functional and interdependent parts, the Mind, Heart and Will. Each of these has three interdependent parts. The Mind has knowledge, understanding and wisdom, the Heart has values, beliefs and attitudes, with the Will having control, choice and gateway.

When an individual struggles with the question of "how do others think and feel about me or toward me", they are extraordinarily vulnerable. Inside their Soul the Heart is carrying values, beliefs and attitudes that support the significance of other people's opinions. In thinking a little about this we can see how the more we give weight to other people's opinions of us, the more vulnerable we are to developing feelings based on what others say, including both verbal and non-verbal communication. Sometimes a disdainful look is more powerful than words at delivering a message. Our internal emotional response to such a look could be shame, or guilt or a sense of inadequacy, and this might prompt us to fall further into our emotional trap.

The basic process going on in this situation of valuing other people's opinions when determining how we feel about ourselves is this. An individual has a set of values, beliefs and attitudes that when combined together give importance to what other people in their lives think and feel about or toward them. The Mind of this individual has a knowledge of these other people, and certain level of understanding and wisdom of and about them. So when one of these other people communicates a message, our individual makes a choice inside their Will and either opens the gateway into their Soul or not.

So, let us say this other person has some level of importance in the individual's life, making the message somewhat important. On top of this the message is one of disrespect, or disapproval, or possibly even of contempt. If we value the other person's opinion and believe it to be true, we could be quite devastated, and go into an emotional tailspin. This might push us to jump into our coping mechanism, like reaching for the bottle, or taking a pill, or even rushing around the house cleaning it until it is perfect.

All of us have experienced where we have received a message from another person, and we've gone into a tailspin, followed by some form of dysfunctional behavior. When these dysfunctional behaviors become a habit or pattern, we are trapped! We are in an emotional prison.

By now, you have realized that I like to use real life normal situations to illustrate a point. I can think of no better example of this point about other people's opinions than peer pressure. Peer pressure operates throughout our lives; none of us is immune. The time where it seems to have the most impact is adolescence, so let's look at a couple of examples of what might be going on in the lives of our teenagers.

How about an academically gifted boy who has trouble making connections with his male classmates? He is not "cool"; he is a nerd and is just plain locked out of all of the cliques. Then one of the "cool" kids throws one of those disparaging remarks at him. It could be something like, "look, here comes straight A Alfie!" Alfie suddenly has a wild thought, "if I don't keep getting an "A" in every class, maybe they'll like me!" So, he deliberately hands in below par work, and is somewhat rebellious in class. He gets a "C", and this gets noticed by the "cool" crowd. Alfie does it again, and his wild thought starts to lead him away from academic excellence and into the "cool" crowd. Our character, Alfie, has discovered that failure leads to the acceptance of those around him.

Inside Alfie's Soul the important values, beliefs and attitudes changed from valuing getting good grades, believing that working hard and having an attitude of excellence was important. They became valuing relationships with the "cool" crowd, believing that failure was necessary and having an attitude of not caring about grades. This was reinforced by the response of the 'cool" crowd, as the peer pressure slowly and remorselessly worked on him.

Now, let us take a look at a young girl, Sandy, who is middle of the road in everything, an okay student, attractive but not stunning, has some friends but isn't usually asked out for a date by boys. She hears tales from her girlfriends of what happens on their dates. It all sounds like fun, and it is exciting to her, and she starts to long for some of these things for herself.

Meet George, he is a little older, and seems to be popular, and has had many girlfriends. Sandy gets introduced to George by one of her friends, and at last she gets asked if she wants to go to the Friday night football game. They agree to meet at the game, and Sandy fantasizes all week about what Friday night is going to be like. It all goes well, they have a great time with their friends at the game and George offers to take her home. She naturally accepts, wanting to be "normal", and George drives them to a secluded place. They talk a little then George kisses her, and she is emotionally swept away. One thing leads to another, as they say, and Sandy is faced with a choice to compromise herself by giving in to his advances or to stick with her principles and risk losing him.

We've all heard this story repeat itself many times in many lives; some of us may even have been a George or a Sandy. In Sandy's Soul a conflict has appeared, she is faced with a choice of violating her values or gaining the acceptance of this boy. Peer pressure started when her girlfriends started to date, and talk about their exploits, explaining how good they felt. Sandy's perception was that she needed to have that too. She wanted to be part of the crowd, and to feel accepted.

These simple examples give us a picture of how easily peer pressure can work on adolescents. We will discuss this more in the next chapter and show how this can lead to the movement of a young person into an emotional prison. Next we move to discussing "responsibility."

Personal Responsibility

This fourth and last major factor in the SPAR approach to looking at what points us toward emotional prisons can be hard to get the Mind around. It revolves around the issue of internal personal accountability, and can be looked at using this question.

How do I feel about myself, due to my ability to meet specific standards?

On the face of it, there seems to be some similarity with the "Performance" factor discussed previously in this chapter. I admit that there is to a limited extent as they both concern our actions. The difference, though, is this. Performance is more about quantitative issues, like how high was my test score, how much do I earn or is my house clean, or behaviors whose outcomes can be easily measured. What I call responsibility is more about qualitative things like, am I helping needy people, am I too materialistic or am I a good person. These are usually highly subjective and difficult to measure, but we all have a sense of if we are meeting specific or particular standards.

We all face subjective standards. Here are some questions or statements that we hear in one form or another that demonstrate what I am beginning to explain.

1. I'm not a good enough mother.
2. I wish I could give some money to "feed the children", but I don't have any spare cash.
3. My yard isn't as pretty as her yard.

4. Why do I have to shop at Wal-Mart instead of Neimans?
5. My parents gave me this crummy Ford, and all my friends have Beamers.

You can see that these types of phrases all relate something personal to some form of external standard. There is, of course, no way for any human living to not be subject to qualitative standards. Every society, every culture and every family has them. Some of these standards are more specific and codified, which we usually call rules or laws, but most are unwritten, and worse than that, they often change over time. This creates a tremendous problem for any person who gets their sense of emotional well being from how perfectly they meet these standards. Let's take a look at what might be happening inside the Soul of such an individual.

For our example here why don't we look at the woman who says, "I'm not a good enough mother." This seems like a statement of fact, but it is not. The woman has dropped a couple of words. She is really emotionally responding to a situation involving her children. A more accurate statement would be, "I feel like I'm not being a good mother." What kinds of emotions could cause someone to feel this way about themselves?

The clearest answer here, in my opinion, is that she feels a sense of inadequacy in her parenting capabilities. There could also be some underlying guilt, shame, disappointment or hurt feelings somewhere. What is going on is that the woman has matched an event or a situation with what she knows in her Mind, and believes or values in her Heart and realizes that things don't add up in some way. It might be that her daughter has informed her that she has gotten pregnant, or that her son has been arrested for dealing drugs at his high school. Or it could be something as innocuous as one of her kids flunking a test. Whatever it is, the woman has compared the situation to a standard, and ended up with negative feelings about herself.

What does she do next? The answer to that depends on what kind of coping mechanisms she has developed over the years. It could be that she rages, or goes into a funk or depressed state. She might go take a Valium or pour herself a stiff drink. After this she feels a little better or her negative feelings have been diminished. This reinforces that the way she deals with distress in her life seems to work, and helps her to slide into her emotional prison.

Let us consider something else here; the variable standard. What if it was socially acceptable for the daughter to be pregnant? Don't laugh, because in our culture, this has become almost expected or normal for some social groups. A mother in this sub group might actually say, "It is about time", and she may not experience any negative emotions. My point here is that even though the event is the same, having a different standard, or set of values and beliefs results in two different motherly reactions. I think I do need to state here that I am not looking at the right and wrong of this. I am only interested in the way one feels as a result of applying whatever standards one lives by.

The point of this section of the chapter, which is sub-titled "responsibility", is to show how our emotional state and particularly how we feel about ourselves is heavily dependent on the standards we apply to our lives. We all have a set of standards that we make ourselves accountable to, which is why I have called this factor responsibility. We are responsible to ourselves for meeting these standards. When we don't meet them, negative feelings often occur in our Soul and these can push us into behaviors or responses that eventually become emotional prisons.

I want to take a moment here to look at a spiritual aspect of this Responsibility factor. We all get our standards from somewhere. It most often begins in the family, then we get new standards fed to us all through life, from our social groups, our workplace, our culture, our legal system, almost everywhere we turn! Generally speaking, if we don't conform to these standards, anarchy reigns. This is true on a national level and on a personal level. If we don't meet our personal standards within our close relationships they have a certain chaotic feel. For example if a husband or wife steps outside of their marriage vows, the family is thrown into disarray.

God took time to try to help us avoid this personal anarchy. He gave us a simple set of standards to live by; we call them "The Ten Commandments." They can be found in the book of Exodus 20:3-17. I am not going to quote them here; I'm just going to comment.

Some people view these commandments as a set of do's and don'ts, which is an incorrect view. God gave them to us for several reasons, the primary one being that since He designed us, He knew what kind of trouble we could get ourselves into. He gave us the commandments, out of His love for us, to help us avoid this personal anarchy in our lives. If we followed the standards He laid out for us, our lives would be much easier, the heartaches fewer and relationships would become more fulfilling.

This is a very practical set of standards, let me show you some examples.

Commandment 7 – Don't commit adultery. If we all kept this, there would be no pregnancies outside of marriage, there would be fewer divorces, there would be less sexually transmitted disease, no addictions to pornography. Isn't that less anarchy?

Commandment 10 – Don't covet your neighbors stuff. What if we did apply this? We wouldn't try to "keep up with the Joneses", we would have less debt, and there would be fewer wars. Also less anarchy.

If we really meditate on these ten standards, we can actually come to understand that they are not for God's benefit, they are for our benefit.

Before we move on I want to give the reader a simple bullet point summary of the SPAR factors.

SPAR Summary

1. Security – Looks at "How do I feel about myself?"
2. Performance – Addresses the question, "How do I feel about myself, due to what I do?"
3. Acceptance – This is about answering the question, "How do others feel about me?"
4. Responsibility – Is a recognition that we all have an internal personal accountability, and that we face the challenge, 'How do I feel about myself, due to my ability to meet specific standards?"

It is these four factors that are primarily responsible for us falling into an emotional prison. There is typically one dominant factor, but some of us may have more than one operating in our lives.

Enough of the theory! Let's move on to applying it in the next two chapters, and using it as we discuss the individual emotional prisons.

9

ADOLESCENCE

Adolescence is that time when I think, it can be- it's the cruelest place on Earth. It can really be heartless.
Tori Amos

In this chapter, I am going to take a look at the period in our lives known as adolescence, and apply the SPAR approach to what are some of the most common observations about that group. I want us to take a look at how some of the teenage behaviors can be explained and understood much better if we look at them through SPAR eyes, than just random guessing about what is going on. First though we ought to agree on what an adolescent is.

Traditionally, adolescence has been thought to begin around 13 years of age and go on until about 19. If we look at some of the older cultures around the world, they seem to have some level of social recognition at that age. Examples are; in the Jewish culture, one of the oldest in existence, the Bar Mitzvah (boys) and the Bat Mitzvah (girls), in Islam they have a circumcision rite for boys, in Buddhism there is a rite called Shinbyu, in ancient Greece there was often an initiation into the military at about 13, and of course Christianity had "confirmation." The point is that all types of nations, peoples and cultures had these rites to recognize a new and more mature phase of life.

The World Health Organization (WHO) which is a special agency of the United Nations has a different definition. In 1995, they modified their view, and now say that adolescence goes from 10 years old to 19. The basic problem with their approach is that they focus mostly on the medical and physiological aspects of this group. I am only really going to consider the psychological perspective in detail, so I'll stick with tradition and use the 13 to 19 years of age boundaries.

It seems to me that it is in this stage of life that we are most vulnerable to becoming long-term prisoners of our own emotions. This is where the seeds of our future life are planted, and they can grow to choke us or grow to help us flourish. In the context of what this book is about, the central question is, "What is going on inside these adolescent Souls?" Let us try to figure it out.

Strictly speaking, a miracle is an event where something supernatural occurs, but sometimes I think that growing up is a miracle. Surely, it is never more evident than in adolescence, where a person goes from being a child to being an adult in just a few years. The enormity of the change is often thought of as mostly a physical occurrence. It involves puberty, physical reshaping, voice changes and as all of us might want to add, raging hormones. Yet, in my opinion, psychological changes, or put in the context of the book, transformations of the operation of the Soul, are even more pronounced.

When reflecting on changes in something, it is often prudent to spend some time on the starting point, so at the risk of seeming tedious I am going to outline the operation of a Soul again.

We have stated the Soul is made up of three parts, with each part having three characteristics, and that the nine total characteristics act on an interdependent basis. These parts and characteristics are:

1. The Mind – Knowledge, Understanding and Wisdom.
2. The Heart – Values, Beliefs and Attitudes.
3. The Will – Choice, Control and Gateway.

In a fully developed Soul, all these nine act in harmony for the benefit of the individual. Whatever situation arises the Soul would use whichever of these characteristics were needed to respond. One of the reasons we bring trouble on ourselves is that our Souls often don't operate in a harmonious way. It is also true that if our Soul is not well developed, like the Soul of an adolescent, we will make less than optimal decisions.

In the adolescent, the Mind, Heart and Will are still a major work in progress. One way to think of it is that the whole process of Soul development is like building a home. During childhood and up to the point of coming into adolescence the foundation and framing of the home are completed. Adolescence is where we start to add the outside walls, roof and interior sheetrock, which is the stage where we can see the home taking a real finite shape. Just for completion of the analogy, adulthood is where we finish off the home with trim and painting and decoration. Adulthood is also when we sometimes have to repaint, do some retrimming and redecorating.

From our analogy we can understand that some basic Soul functions are in place as a person enters adolescence. Things like communicating, analyzing and problem solving are Soul skills that are present, even if they have not become fully developed. Other important Soul skills that have not developed well up to this point are self-control, healthy choices and an orderly gateway. This is where the adolescent begins their work.

I've heard a parent or two say something like, "When she turned thirteen, the light switch of reasonableness got turned off, and it didn't get switched back on until she was twenty!" I personally prefer a different approach. I look at this as a light switch turning on, not off. It is the light switch of "self", and over the next few pages we are going to look at what that means.

Some Characteristics of the Adolescent Years

Hopefully, we can all remember some of the period in our lives that we call adolescence, and some of the experiences we had. Maybe some of us will connect with the list I am about to write down, and remember how we were. This is meant to be a list of developmental characteristics found in adolescents, which we will refer to later.

1. Disillusionment, disenchantment or disappointment.
2. Becoming increasingly dishonest and deceptive.
3. Denial of actual emotions, and substitution of others.
4. Avoid responsibility and commitment.
5. Become more self-centered, self-conscious and self-reliant.
6. Increasingly influenced by others.

I'm sure it is possible to add more to the list, but I think this list will serve the purpose of trying to understand what happens inside the Soul of the adolescent. Notice that all the items on the list are about self or something that affects the individual internally and personally.

There is something even more profound than the self aspect of this list. All of these items are related to the Heart! They all involve values, beliefs and attitudes. Do you recall that earlier in the chapter I said that I thought that this was the period in our lives when we were most likely to be vulnerable to becoming long-term prisoners of our emotions? Now, from inspecting the list, we can see why!

94

Processing Inside the Soul of an Adolescent

Going back to our "building a house" analogy, the adolescent is at a major disadvantage in trying to process life's situations. He or she is trying to use a hammer to nail down shingles when the right tool might be a nail gun. They are trying to put the bricks up to build a wall without using mortar, and they are trying to float sheetrock without a level. It is plainly amateur hour! This is because, of course, they have a relatively underdeveloped Soul, an immature Soul.

What is so immature about it? The short answer is practically everything! They have only been living a few years and so don't have the benefit of extensive knowledge, understanding or wisdom about much of life. Their values, beliefs and attitudes are probably those of their parents, with some input from their social groups and extended family. Even though adolescents have some values, beliefs and attitudes, they aren't set in concrete, as they haven't really had them tested by life to any great extent. The self-control and choices they exhibit are also a function of either obedience or compliance with family norms or rules. The gateway of the Will has mostly been open to anything as children, and so hasn't really had an opportunity to function under the individual's volitional care.

There is a verse of Scripture that comes to Mind when I think about adolescence, the period of time when we start to really test our beliefs. It is taken from the book of James, and it is the concluding verse of a short instruction on receiving wisdom in faith (belief in the unseen or unknown). Let's read it; James 1:8:

Being a double-minded man, unstable in all his ways.

I placed this verse here to provide us with a working definition of the operation of the Soul of an adolescent. This does not mean that they are mentally deranged or obtuse. It does provide a word picture of where our adolescents find themselves. They have a lot of internal Soul conflict, they are not sure about things, and they are still learning. The instability is clearly demonstrated when we see how they can respond one way to a situation today, and tomorrow they react totally differently.

Now I've laid the groundwork to be able to take a closer look at what might be going on inside the Soul of our teens. Starting with the Mind we can probably make a statement that the adolescent arrives at the age of thirteen with a reasonably well-organized Mind. His or her knowledge, understanding and wisdom have developed to the point of a fair amount of maturity. By this time of their life they have accumulated, through being taught, a general understanding of how to behave in most circumstances and the wisdom to apply what they know.

In the Heart, as I've said earlier, the adolescent has values, beliefs and attitudes that reflect what they have picked up from mostly the parents, but also from others. In the Will, control and choice have some order to them, as the child tends to comply with or obey the parents. The gateway has been open to all influences up to this point. It is in the Heart and Will that the big changes in adolescence occur. Let's look at them.

When a child reaches adolescence he or she comes to an unconscious realization that they are actually in charge of their own Soul. This is the light switch being turned on to Self that I discussed earlier. It essentially occurs within the Will, where the three characteristics change in emphasis, which is part of every person's maturing process. Let's identify these changes.

1. The choice characteristic alters its focus from making choices that fit in with family or social norms, to choices that the adolescent makes for their own perceived benefit.
2. The control attribute goes from being centered on control for or by parents, or other significant people, to being all about what the Self wants. It might be better called self-centered-control at this time.
3. The gateway, which has been so open through the childhood years, becomes closed more often as the adolescent chooses and controls what he or she lets in or out of the Soul.

While this simple and probably obvious set of changes happens in the adolescent's Will, it is the effect it has on the Heart that is important.

The adolescent comes into his or her teen years with a set of values, beliefs and attitudes obtained through all the influences of their short life. Most of them will be from their family of origin. For example if the parents have a value that it is always good to wear clean clothes, then it is likely that the child will have the same value. Or maybe the parents believe that God doesn't exist, the adolescent will be a budding atheist too. If the young person comes from a family that has an attitude of superiority, then the adolescent is likely to be a snob as well.

96

What happens in the Soul of the adolescent is that these values, beliefs and attitudes suddenly become challenged. The young person is getting in touch with the unconscious realization that they are actually in charge of their own Soul. This is an enormous shift in perception of who they are. It is the time when the Soul moves from being intertwined with the significant people around it to becoming independent. It is the time when this adolescent Soul goes from being protected to becoming vulnerable. This vulnerability is particularly acute because the adolescent hasn't developed many internal protective mechanisms that help him or her to cope with life's challenges.

As the adolescent opens and closes his or her gateway to new and alternative ideas or views of life, slowly and surely their previous values, beliefs and attitudes are confronted. They are confronted by their teachers, by their peers, by the media and by their social groups. These old values, beliefs and attitudes are tested and attacked such that the teen begins to question almost everything around them. The biggest questions are, who am I and how do I feel about myself? This is because they are internally beginning to separate themselves from their previous situation as a child, and becoming more aware that they are an individual having personal meaning and value.

Adolescence is also the period in life that we see the beginning of a human's ability to hold two or more different beliefs around the same subject. Because of the bombardment of new or alternative belief possibilities the Heart gets to the point where it can simply hold two conflicting beliefs around the same issue. The easy example is that of teen sexuality. A teen may have the family value that says no sex until marriage, and also believe that oral sex is acceptable because it is not "actual sex." If we consider that an adolescent may be dealing with many beliefs in this way, is it any wonder that they seem so conflicted and confused?

I now want to take a look at the Soul activity behind the six development characteristics of adolescents that I identified earlier in the chapter, and I'm going to do it by applying the SPAR method from the previous chapter.

The Effect of Personal Security in the Adolescent

Each of us asks this question from time to time. How do I feel about myself? Mostly, we are not necessarily in touch with this question, or our answer, in a deliberate or meditative way. This question and answer for the adolescent, however, is one of the keys to how they conduct their life, and if they head toward an emotional prison.

Up to the point of adolescence, an individual is in their "child" mode. What they think of themselves, how they feel about themselves and how they act is mostly a function of their identity within the family. When adolescence arrives the Self switch gets turned on. The adolescent is awakened to the fact that he or she is a separate person from others. The Soul of the teen goes from being heavily influenced, and therefore controlled, by close people, to becoming less influenced by them. Those of us who have experienced raising teens understand this, as it sometimes seems like our teens are out of control. Well, they are, they are out of our influence and control, and have become self-guided individuals.

Unfortunately for the adolescent, they are usually not ready for this new "self-guided" phase of their life. This question, "How do I feel about myself?" becomes amazingly hard to answer. Without direction from the parents or close family, the teen is a rudderless boat. He or she goes wherever the wind blows.

Inside the Soul of the adolescent, the orderliness of family life is replaced by the chaos of immature self-control. At the beginning of this time the Mind of the teen is well ordered, changes in what the teen knows and understands come slowly, and his or her accumulated wisdom, which has been acquired from the family, continues to serve the teen well. It is in the Heart and Will where the problems begin to surface.

As I mentioned earlier, the gateway of the Will of the adolescent becomes opened and closed in a more self-directed way. This allows new information, different ideas and fresh life approaches into the Soul. The problem for the teen, though, is that they cannot distinguish between healthy and unhealthy input. The results of this are chaos and confusion inside the Heart.

The values, beliefs and attitudes that exist in the Heart coming into adolescence are under constant attack. For example, if a teen believes God exists when they are 13 years old, it is likely that the "God exists" belief will be challenged directly and indirectly almost every day. It has to be incredibly hard for a teen to stand firm in any value, belief or attitude they carried into adolescence. With all the attacking going on, a state of chaos and confusion exists.

By now, you have probably acquired a good idea as to how difficult it is for a teen to answer the question, "How do I feel about myself?" The reality is that he or she doesn't have a consistent answer, and at times may not even know. Is it any wonder teens as a group tend to be extraordinarily insecure about themselves?

Let's take a short look at what this state of Soul chaos and confusion does to adolescents in the context of the six characteristics that I specified earlier.

There is a 3D effect - Disillusionment, disenchantment or disappointment. I think that it is very likely a shock to the Soul of a teen when the breakpoint of child to adolescent is reached. They are no longer, mommy's little boy, or daddy's little girl, they are Jason and Jennifer. Their identity is fundamentally changed from their own internal perspective. Whatever their belief was about this has to change in the light of new facts coming through the gateway of their Soul and a new subconscious understanding of their separateness.

This change must be appreciated for what it is; radical. Thinking and feeling one way about yourself in the child phase of your life, is replaced by thinking and feeling other ways about who you are as an adolescent. I've called these changes radical, because they are. Is it any wonder that with all the uncertainty brought on by radical changes that a teen might become disillusioned about whom they are and how they feel about themselves. It really ought not to surprise us when a teen learns that certain chemicals or behaviors alter (at least for a time) these negative feelings. That is when an increased openness to some compulsive behaviors that ultimately put a person into an emotional prison can appear.

Next let's look at the developmental characteristic of becoming increasingly dishonest and deceptive. I'm not sure this is particularly relevant for the "How do I feel about myself?" question we are looking at here. It becomes more important later as we look at the Performance, Acceptance and Responsibility sections below. It does dovetail into the next characteristic covering denial of feelings and substituting other emotions.

The third developmental characteristic is highly important though. It is, denial of actual emotions, and substitution of others. This is actually a problem for all of us, not just adolescents. The root of the problem lies with the inability to identify what we might be feeling in any particular situation. Every person who reads this book has experienced this. For the adolescent, this is a major problem.

Denial of experiencing an emotion occurs either consciously or sub-consciously; which way doesn't really matter, the effect is the same. We substitute a different emotion. To be sure we understand this accurately I want to say this clearly. In the Soul of the adolescent a feeling may arise, and the teen sometimes chooses to substitute a different emotion. The original feeling is still there, in the Soul, and is not resolved or dealt with, and can be thought of as, being stuffed down to be dealt with another time.

An example could be if a teen feels rejected over some issue. He or she may choose to substitute happiness because they weren't chosen. Crazy, yes, but understandable if we think about it as a coping mechanism. We must remember that the teen is no longer under the full emotional protection of the family since the Self switch has been turned on. Decisions on how to deal with feelings that arise in day-to-day life have started to be handled by the adolescent and their immature Soul.

I think it is also good for us to look at a few more examples of how emotion substitution is played out in teenage life.

1. Driving – I feel better about myself when I speed. I ignore a sense of being unsafe and substitute a feeling of euphoria.
2. Drinking/Drugs – I can handle life better when I'm using. I ignore my inability to make quality decisions and substitute a feeling of nothing matters much.
3. Sex – It feels good to do this, I'm excited. I ignore the sense that I'm using someone to meet my needs, and substitute feelings of personal exhilaration, or maybe acceptance.

There are many, many examples that can be written here, but the point is simple. Teenagers are not capable, because they are not ready, of identifying their emotions well, and will often substitute a false (unfelt) emotion for a real one. The big one, of course, is how do they feel about themselves, and they can often substitute "I feel strong" with "I feel weak", or maybe, "I feel loved" with "I'm not accepted."

One of the results of this is that the adolescent will sometimes turn to some way of dealing with all the Soul chaos this leads to, and this can put them on track to an emotional prison.

The next characteristic is that of avoiding responsibility and commitment. This issue doesn't seem to relate much to the 'How do I feel about myself" question, but will be important later on, and I'll cover it then. The only thing that crosses my Mind on this is the thought that the teen wants to avoid connecting feeling secure, and how responsible they might be, as they are unsure of themselves.

Characteristic number five is, "Become more self-centered, self-conscious and self-reliant." The whole chapter revolves around this. Every adolescent is trying to get to the bottom line on the issue of who they are, and they all have their Self switch turned on. They are becoming "self-everything" as they work toward understanding their own identity, and how they feel about themselves. Everything they do, their actions and their words, is done to drive their Soul toward knowing who they are. Even when they are "doing for others" as in volunteer work, they are still operating in Self mode.

I know this next statement may cause disagreement in the Minds of some readers, but that doesn't make if less true! We are all designed to go through the process of human growth. And that is, conception, birth, childhood, adolescence and adulthood. We are made to find out who we are through understanding how we feel about ourselves in between childhood and adulthood. This is true for all peoples, cultures, belief systems or whatever way we want to categorize ourselves. Think about it. It is in our teen years that we make life-long decisions on what we believe about ourselves, or who we are. This emphatic statement doesn't preclude the understanding that we can't change how we perceive ourselves later in life, but it is much more difficult to change our internal belief systems when we slip into adulthood. This is why there is a worldwide focus, present in all cultures, on cementing beliefs in the teenage years.

In the western world the Self orientation of adolescents is accepted and even encouraged. It is approached through a culture that has derived most of its values from Christianity, which values the acceptance and individuality of a person. In other places, for example, the Moslem world, or the oriental cultures, individuality is discouraged, and is replaced with more submissive demands on the teen. The result is that in western society the teen tries to find out who they are, and how they feel about themselves and then fits into the social fabric. In the other cultures the teen is told what their identity is by the culture itself, with the result that the issue of who they are, and how they feel about themselves never seems to get resolved. (Or put another way, the pressure is to conform to the cultural values, not be a person in your own right.)

I have a certain sense of sadness when I write about this diminishment of Self in other cultures. This is because I value the freedom to choose to be who you are. When one looks at things like creativity, prosperity and diversity one can see that the western world has an unmatched superiority. This all begins right here, in how our adolescents are able to deal with the question of Self, or "who am I" or "How do I feel about myself." When a teen knows who they are and how they feel about themselves, they can then mature beyond "self." This allows them to develop into a person who uses their own abilities and passions in life. Also, since their Soul knows who they are, they can move to the higher moral plane of serving others, voluntarily, instead of in compliance with the family or cultural edicts.

The last teen characteristic is that of becoming increasingly influenced by others. This will be more appropriately dealt with under the subject of acceptance below.

The Effect of Personal Performance in the Adolescent

As a reminder I want to lay out the question that we are looking at when we discuss personal performance. It is, "How do I feel about myself, due to what I do?" It is in the adolescent years that this question starts to take on significance. This is the time when Self takes over, as we have discussed before, and this is true for how we do, as in perform, in our teen years. It is the time when we begin to stand or fall on the basis of our own decisions, our own talents and our own motivations.

The very human problem of our reaction to our own success or failure begins to loom large in our Souls during adolescence. I want to take a look at this in terms of a sport called soccer, which the rest of the world calls football. This is one of the most merit-oriented sports there is. There are no substitutes for the talents you need to succeed at every level. For a teen that engages in this sport it is a major test for the question, "How do I feel about myself, based on what I do?"

There are many skills needed, some physical and others Soul-related. The major physical abilities include athleticism, speed, ball to foot coordination, leg strength, spatial awareness and stamina. Soul skills include, knowledge of the rules, assessing opponents, reading game flow, assertiveness in entanglements and timing of exertion. To do well, a great deal of talent has to be present.

From my description of these abilities, we can see that there is a lot of room for not making the cut at all levels of the sport. Now add in the fact that it is the most popular sport in the world, and teens that love soccer are set up for a Soul problem. For the purpose of this discussion, let us assume that we are going to deal with boys.

If a boy grows up as a soccer fan, he wants to emulate the great players, but what if he can't? What if he can't even make his high school team? Then it is entirely possible that he will experience a sense of failure or at least a sense of inadequacy. What does he do with this? He is now probably too old to go to his parents, his peer group will laugh at him, or maybe he could get some counseling from the coach over dealing with these feelings. No, it doesn't happen that way: The teen is alone, and has to resolve the negative feeling somehow, or it gets stuffed down for another time.

What is most likely is that the teen will find another outlet for his energy and his unresolved feelings. He could turn anywhere. It could be trying harder to make the team; it could be that he will take up computer games, or it might be chasing girls, or alcohol and drugs, it might even be religion.

From this simple look at soccer, we can see that this thinking can be applied to all adolescents in the things they try to do. We could apply it to schoolwork, sports, relationships, music, or anything they get involved in. The problem here is not the actual performance; it is how the teen feels about himself or herself as a result of it. How the adolescent deals with that question will be a determining factor in their propensity to fall into an emotional prison.

In terms of the developmental characteristics outlined earlier we can see that a young person could easily become disillusioned with their life if personal performance is important to them. We can also see how they might become more self-conscious about their lack of ability in some way, and how they might choose to run away from life. Escape from the bad feelings is made possible in many ways, and they can all result in a teen being pointed to an emotional trap.

The Effect of Personal Acceptance in the Adolescent

The issue of acceptance from others in the life of an adolescent is huge, and we are going to look at why and what it can do to a teen's life. First let's remind ourselves of the question that is being asked inside the Soul of every teen. "How do I feel about myself, due to my perception of what others feel and think about me?" This is also asked like this, "How do others feel about me?"

As has been said before there is a time during the maturing process of a person when they move from childhood to adolescence. I have described that as a sort of "aha" moment when a Self switch is turned on. Our context here is the subject of how accepted an adolescent feels and what it does to him or her. In this light, I want to take a look at some of the significant and relevant changes which occur as this switch goes on.

The first change concerns protection, by this I mean protection of the Soul. In the early years the parents or other significant people are looking out for the well being of the child. They typically try to keep them away from detrimental influences and when the child is experiencing difficult emotions they are there to help them get resolved. The Soul is being nurtured. When the child gets to adolescence things change, even if the adult guardians don't want it to! The new adolescent starts to allow other influences in through the gateway of the Soul, resulting in new internal challenges to the values, attitudes and beliefs of the immature Soul. The adolescent has only limited abilities at being able to protect their Soul, particularly the Heart.

Next we can consider processing of emotions. The child has, for the most part, grown up being able to express and share their feelings, most obviously inside the family. This allows the emotions to be explored and understood resulting in resolution or the letting go of the feelings. When the teen years start there is a noticeable movement away from expressing and sharing. This is due to the Self switch directing the teen into trying to figure things out for themselves. Of course, they really have only their childhood experiences to draw on, and so without guidance they flounder in trying to resolve things. This can lead to a significant amount of frustration and other negative feelings, which often end up as outward displays of anger, or sometimes these feelings are inwardly held or stuffed. As these negative emotions are not dealt with, they start to build, and can become the starting point for some kind of compulsive behavior. An example might be that a young girl notices that eating food seems to calm her down and she feels better. The result is the beginning of a weight problem.

Now we can look at what I call moving targets. In the early years the adults determine most things for the child: what TV programs are watched, what clothes are worn, what food is eaten, what people you can have as friends, etc. In adolescence that all stops, and the whole cultural shift of the teen years begins. Now the Soul is seeking its own preferences through the exercise of the Will characteristic "choice." The teen picks out new friends, different clothes and selects alternative music and movies. However, there is an underlying problem for the teen. The teen is maturing in his or her personal tastes and the teen's peer group has a very fluid set of unwritten rules on what is "in" or "out." The sum of these two things is what I have called a moving target. The result is a fantastically dynamic situation, and it is hard for a teen to distinguish between what is good for them or not and what is acceptable or not to the group that they may be part of.

Lastly, I want to take a look at belief conflicts. During childhood, beliefs are whatever the family says they are, with the child having very little reason to challenge or doubt them. During adolescence this changes. As has been said before, the Soul becomes open to whole new belief systems, and the world delivers them! One inevitable result of this is that a conflict goes on in the Heart of a teen, a conflict between all the beliefs which he or she is exposed to. Some simple examples are, creation and evolution, respect or disrespect of adults, modest dress or revealing dress, and working or playing in school. Every belief is at risk! This can be quite a problem for an immature Soul to deal with.

We are now ready to look at this Acceptance problem in adolescents.

As a teen moves from childhood to adolescence they move from being protected, supported, and comforted by their family of origin to a place of separation from these things. The highly comfortable place of childhood carries with it a high level of acceptance from the family. I've heard this said this way, "Everybody knows their place." Then as the adolescent is thrust into his or her teen years, they are suddenly on their own. The time of normally constant and consistent loving acceptance of them just the way they are is over. It becomes replaced by the harsh realities of life as a teen. Instead of being surrounded by a relatively peaceful, emotionally stable situation, the teen is encircled by peers who don't have a clue about how to accept one another. It is one of those "blind leading the blind" situations.

(I want to remind the reader that this is normal, it is part of the maturing process that is built into all people.)

Picture this situation like this. Adolescence involves a group of people who are trying to interact with each other with at least these four Soul millstones hanging around their necks. They are unprotected, they haven't learned how to process emotions adequately, they have to deal with the moving targets of almost daily changing norms of teen culture and most of their important beliefs are under bombardment. When I look at it from a vantage point way beyond the teen years, it seems like a recipe for insanity.

Is it any wonder that as soon as a teen finds a person or small group where they have at least some relief from the confusion of this "recipe" that they cling to it? To the teen, this is acceptance! This group provides at least some sense of order, of control over life and most importantly it provides relationships. These relationships, to a certain extent, are substitutes for what used to exist in the family. I think it is important here to state that the family has in no way failed. The move of a teen from a totally family-based orientation to a combination family/peer group orientation is part of the designed way an individual grows up.

I think that we ought to get at the root issue here for the adolescent. Inside the family of origin, there is relational certainty. I'm not suggesting everything is perfect, but I am stating that a teen knows where they fit, relationally speaking, with the other family members. They are able to connect with their parents and siblings, aunts and uncles, and other family members and feel accepted. In actuality, the teen accepts the level of acceptance within the family as normal and adequate, even if others might say it wasn't.

This normality and adequacy of the level of acceptance then becomes less relevant to the inner working of the adolescent Soul as the child to teen transition takes place. The adolescent suddenly finds they are in an "acceptance wilderness" as they haven't figured out where they are relationally to their peers. This is experienced as rejection! This is then followed by a troublesome, and probably unconscious, realization that they really aren't connected with the people they hang out with. The final resting place of this aspect of life is in fear, fear of rejection. It is this fear of rejection that becomes the seed of some new behaviors as the teen seeks to gain acceptance. Some of these behaviors can lead them, over time, into addictive issues and emotional prisons. A simple example could be that a girl becomes promiscuous because she is seeking the acceptance she needs through giving her body away.

I personally believe that every person experiences rejection and the fear of rejection in significant ways throughout their life. As I said earlier in the book, I was abandoned in my childhood. As a result I carry the fear of rejection around with me, and it is now about 50 years later.

The fear of rejection and the six developmental characteristics.

Let's look at this adolescent fear of rejection as it relates to the six developmental characteristics we listed earlier in the chapter. These are; disillusionment, increasing dishonesty, denial of emotions, avoidance of responsibility, more self-centeredness and increasing influence of others.

It is easy to see how an adolescent who is experiencing either rejection or the fear of it could become disillusioned with life. After all, their basic need for relationship is no longer being met. It is also easy to imagine how, in extreme cases, a person might even become so despairing that suicide is actually seen as a way out of the pain of rejection.

Sometimes a teen discovers that lying to others helps with this rejection. He or she might lie to their parents about how they are doing in their life. It stops the parent from pursuing questions about the teen's friendships or lack of them. It could be easier to lie to their peers about something to make themslef more important, and therefore have some level of acceptance. The more lying works for a teen, the more he or she will do it.

Denial of emotions is a big deal in the area of acceptance. Denying fear of rejection is the obvious one, but there are more that go along with it. Consider the problem of not feeling adequate or being ashamed of oneself, and maybe being lonely. These are powerful emotional forces inside the Soul of a teen, and they require powerful counter-forces if the teen is to feel better. The obvious route, and the one most frequently taken, is that of anger. Without getting into deep psychology I just want to say that anger is usually the result of a deepening and also joining of other emotions. Anger is a secondary emotion. It is likely that the teen first experiences things like hurt, pain or frustration, and these end up as anger. Have you ever noticed how angry even the most levelheaded teen can get? It could be rejection working its ugly way through them.

With growing up comes an awesome responsibility of taking care of oneself. For the teen this is not easy and they are not ready, even though some of them think they are. This is particularly true of taking care of the Soul. Just like avoiding doing the laundry, the teen will avoid working on his or her Soul needs. Things like the determination of personal values, attitudes and beliefs are not given adequate and appropriate attention. The need for personal acceptance from others pushes these things onto the back burner. The pursuit of acceptance, and the fear of rejection can even cause the teen to push aside healthy values, attitudes and beliefs in favor of ones that gain him or her more acceptance.

Self-centeredness is the fifth developmental characteristic; when a child becomes an adolescent, the Self switch is turned on. In the area of acceptance or fear of rejection it is all about getting the fear dealt with. Very quickly the teen will discover that he or she is mostly alone, particularly if they choose to not include their parents in dealing with this fear. This means that many of their actions will be about this and will be self-centered. An example could be when the teen sneaks out at night to meet up with his or her friends for some social reason.

The final developmental characteristic is "the increasing influence of others." I find this somewhat obvious. A teen knows that when they do whatever it takes to fit in with the group, they feel accepted. Therefore they openly allow the group members to influence them and their choices. I just wonder how many teens have died in traffic wrecks because they allowed their friends to influence them into drinking and driving.

As we can see, the power of acceptance and rejection in the life of a teen is formidable. Not being able to handle rejection, which will always come into every life, points people toward emotional prisons. It is not a subtle thing either, it is pervasive, it is consuming and it is dangerous for our adolescents. The only truly successful way I have seen in dealing with this is a belief in God and what He says. In Romans 15:7 it says this:

Therefore, accept one another, just as Christ also accepted us to the glory of God.

God accepts us just as we are, and we do not need to have another human being's acceptance or approval. We are obviously instructed to accept one another, but that is because we are to emulate Jesus, not to make the other person feel better about themselves. If you are a teen and this belief that you are accepted, no matter what, is in your Heart, you are likely to be less vulnerable to the fear of rejection and all the problems it can bring.

The Effect of Personal Responsibility in the Adolescent

I want to remind us here that this subject of what I call "Personal Responsibility" can be a little difficult to appreciate. It revolves around the question, "How do I feel about myself, due to my ability to meet certain standards?" It involves the issue of how am I doing compared to some subjective values I may be trying to live by. An example could be, "Am I a good person?" So now we come to the point of looking at adolescents trying to deal with subjective standards and how they feel about themselves as a result of them, or their ability to meet them.

Can you imagine being a teenager and hearing words like these, "You're just not cool?" How devastated could you be? I have never been able to figure out what "being cool," meant. That is because it is a subjective standard! It is a standard that so many teens want to be able to reach, but nobody can objectively explain what it is. It is one of those moving targets I talked about earlier.

Being cool, of course, involves the issue of acceptance and rejection, which we have covered. However it, and other subjective standards, can lead to other emotional responses. What if I wanted to be cool because I was driven to achieve in all things? I might as a teen try my best to be cool because when I finally am cool I have a sense of personal satisfaction or even elatedness. But, there is a downside.

Being cool, or any other subjective standard, is illusory, and that is because it is a moving target. Being cool at 14 years old is not the same as being cool at 15; the standard changes. This can lead to many potentially damaging emotional responses such as inadequacy, frustration, shame and pain. As we have seen before, an adolescent will often start into a behavior that ultimately leads to an emotional prison, just to feel better, emotionally speaking.

Let's stay with the being cool example and look at the six developmental characteristics. First comes disillusionment; this is easy to see. If you are not cool, how long will it take to come to a place in your Heart where you believe you will never be cool? You have become disillusioned! Apply this thought process in imagining that a teen may have ten or more subjective standards that they are trying to meet. When we do that we can see how this can lead to major disillusionment.

The second characteristic of "Becoming increasingly dishonest" is a creeping problem for the teen when dealing with the issue of subjective standards. This is because these kinds of things are often highly internalized. By this I mean that while the origin of a subjective value may be some source outside of the Soul, such as a peer or a teen magazine, it is taken in through the gateway of the Will and settles in the Heart. When it gets there, the adolescent matches it against the knowledge gained through life, then also connects it to his or her beliefs and determines if the standard is relevant and/or important.

This is where the dishonesty starts. A teen discovers that a subjective standard or value is important to him or her, but that it doesn't fit well with their internal beliefs. The gap between the applicable internal beliefs or values in the teen's Heart and this new subjective value is a "gap of truth." Unless this gap of truth is resolved by throwing out the new subjective value, the gap can only get filled with a lie. So that is what most adolescents will do in response to the gap; they lie! Once the lying begins, it seems to accelerate as the teen becomes increasingly dishonest. At first the lies are internal, or said another way, the teen lies to themselves. Eventually they become external as the teen lies to those around them.

Let's look at being cool again. What if an adolescent is trying to be part of the cool crowd, and it requires listening to certain types of music that has lyrics that demean others or inflame violence. He or she believes that this music is important to their "coolness", but also may believe it is wrong to demean others. The gap of truth is that the lyrics are both cool and objectionable at the same time. So what do they do? First, they deny the truth about the music; that is, of course, the first lie and it is an internal choice they make. Then they tell other teens in the in-crowd that they think it is cool. That is the second level of lies. Then when non-cool people like parents or siblings point out the nature of the music, they lie again, the third level! This third level is serious stuff. They deny that the music is objectionable; they may deny that they like it, and they may even deny that they listen to it.

We can see from my simple example that the teen can slip very easily into a life of denial and lies. Now picture the situation that an adolescent faces; they have many, many subjective standards to deal with. Once the life of denial starts it is almost certain to begin a possibly lifelong problem with gaps of truth. This means that when they get into some form of emotional prison like an addiction, they are in serious trouble! Not being able to see the truth about problems and lying about them, which I have called denial, means that they are very likely to get stuck, because they cannot even start accepting help.

I'm going to skip "Denial of emotions" here as it has been well covered before, but I'll say a few words about avoiding responsibility and commitment. Usually the adolescent that is driven to meet subjective standards will not have a commitment issue, because as far as is possible, they will do whatever it takes to get to those standards. Like a lot of what the teen deals with, this has a downside.

When a boy or girl cannot meet subjective standards easily, negative feelings about oneself can arise. As more and more difficulty is experienced, a teen can slip into times of irresponsibility and exhibit lack of commitment in achieving certain standards. This can even bleed over into their whole life, with the result that things like schoolwork and relationships suffer, possibly resulting in some kind of self-imposed isolation. Often, as this failure to commit and be responsible results in bad grades or losing friends, somebody else gets blamed! I'm sure we have all heard things like, "it was the teacher's fault", or "my friends don't call me anymore." The end point of a "blaming" mentality is an acceptance of failure as a lifestyle. This allows the teen to slip into behaviors that at least temporarily soothe his or her Soul problems, and they get pointed in the direction of an emotional prison.

The next to last characteristic to look at is "Becoming increasingly self-centered, self-conscious and self-reliant." Well, it doesn't take a rocket scientist to see that chasing after subjective standards to feel good about oneself is all about self. Using our "being cool" example shows us that a teen is totally self-centered and very self-conscious as he or she tries to establish their "coolness." Success in this leads to a sense of personal superiority, resulting in increasing self-reliance.

The last characteristic is; "Increasingly influenced by others." As an adolescent moves through the teen years his or her subjective standards come more and more from peers and the popular culture. Being cool is a great example of this. A teen goes from being reliant on his or her immediate family to allowing friends or things like MTV to determine what being cool actually means. In fact, it is imperative that the teen looks to others to determine standards, because of the acceptance problem we covered earlier. Once a tolerable level of acceptance has been reached, the challenge is then to be the coolest or as cool as possible. Some of our teens are seemingly wired to be as cool as possible.

Chasing after these subjective standards often leads to more risky behavior than some teens would wish to engage in. Being cool for some teens might mean doing more drugs, or binge drinking, or mugging others and maybe worst of all, murdering innocent people. Scary, isn't it? That is the power of feeling okay about yourself, or not!

Summarizing the chapter

I seem to have had a lot to say in this chapter, and it is appropriate. I believe through my own and others' experiences that the teen years are our most vulnerable, in the context of emotional prisons.

An adolescent is a person who has been pushed out into the sea of life, but doesn't have complete instructions on how to run the ship. They go from being given plenty of help from his or her crew (the family) to being a lone sailor. The Self switch is now on. How a teen feels about themselves is determined by so many crosscurrents and rip tides. He or she has to deal with being accepted, often called the fear of rejection. Some other major things that get in the way of smooth sailing are the chaos and confusion of an immature Soul, fear of failure and changing subjective standards.

I can't help but be reminded of a simple suggestion from the "Book of Wisdom" which we call Proverbs:

Prov 22:6 - Train up a child in the way he should go, even when he is old he will not depart from it.

In the context of this chapter it says to me to get your children ready by teaching them strong values, beliefs and attitudes, things that will see them through the adolescent years. That is how you can help protect them when they start to experience the adolescent pressures we have talked about. A well-built faith system will do more to keep your child safe in adolescence than lectures, grounding or other punishments.

Having covered the teen, we are now ready to look at what comes next, early adulthood.

10

EARLY ADULTHOOD

What is an adult? A child blown up by age.
Simone De Beauvoir

We have just finished looking at that period of life which we call adolescence, in which I used the nominal ages of 13 to 19 as boundary markers. Now we come to the next phase, early adulthood. I am going to look at this as the period of time when we begin to make adult choices, and generally speaking it goes from around age 18 or 19 to around 25 for most people.

This period of our lives is characterized by the choices that are made, which are often mostly permanent in nature. The kinds of choices I'm talking about are; whom we are going to pair up with for marriage; what we are going to do after high school (college or enter the workforce) and what career path we might take. Then also, directly springing from one of these choices, we make at least two more significant choices; where we live and whom we socialize with.

Using the SPAR analysis approach I am going to look at how these choices are made and discuss how they can head us toward an emotional prison. For convenience I am going to put these choices into a simple list:

1. Pairing off
2. Further Education
3. Career
4. Location
5. Social group

Transition from adolescence to early adulthood

Before we get down to more detail on this list I want to take some time looking at the transition we make as we go from adolescence to young adulthood. As I start to do this I am reminded of a small nugget of truth found in the greatest sermon ever preached, the Sermon on the Mount. The whole sermon is found in the book of Matthew, and goes from the beginning of chapter 5 to the end of chapter 7. (If you haven't looked at it lately, you might want to read it now.) Right at the end Jesus lays out a major spiritual principle which has application for every person, believer or not.

Mt 7:24-27 - Therefore everyone who hears these words of Mine and acts on them, may be compared to a wise man who built his house on the rock. And the rain fell, and the floods came, and the winds blew and slammed against that house; and yet it did not fall, for it had been founded on the rock. Everyone who hears these words of Mine and does not act on them, will be like a foolish man who built his house on the sand. The rain fell, and the floods came, and the winds blew and slammed against that house; and it fell — and great was its fall.

A Christian who is familiar with this passage will rightly say that it is a piece of advice from Jesus on how to conduct life, which is to build your life around Him and His teachings. However, even a non-Christian can acknowledge that there is basic truth in this passage. Build your life around and on solid principles, and when hard times come you will be able to deal with them. This has direct application here. Let me explain.

We have explored how a child becomes an adolescent, the switch of Self gets turned on. This young person is suddenly in charge of his or her own Soul, but they haven't yet developed the coping skills necessary to operate it. To varying degrees the adolescent experiences what I called "Soul chaos and confusion." This situation can often lead the immature Soul in the direction of some form of coping behavior, meaning they find a way of dealing with the emotional uncertainty that comes along for them. Examples are drugs and alcohol, promiscuous sex and isolating. For a few of these unfortunate young people this heads them into some form of emotional prison.

It is quite plain to all of us that some teens sail through to young adulthood. So why do some get through and some not? The answer is found in the solid principles idea laid out for us by Jesus in His sermon. These principles are the time tested basic truths of life. While it is not the function in any way for this book to instruct parents in child rearing, I would still like to simply list a few of the principles that help a teen get through without experiencing the worst of life in the teen years.

1. Family connection - not turning away from the values the family of origin possesses.

2. Communicate - with the people who have already demonstrated love and caring through the early years.
3. Honesty - sharing of thoughts and feelings with safe people.
4. Avoiding people pleasing - staying away from the trap of always doing things for others at the expense of your well-being.
5. Good company - restricting close friends to those who demonstrate good choices and habits.
6. Faith - maintaining an active and healthy belief system that acknowledges God and His instructions as necessary for high moral standards.

I know that last one might not be totally acceptable to some people. For me though, I know that if I had done these things listed above, particularly the last one, it would have saved me a lot of grief. The point of all this is simple. If a teen has not practiced the good characteristics listed above, they are more than likely to be either in or on their way into an emotional prison. They have built their house, meaning their life, on shifting sands, things like fear of rejection, self-medication of feelings and hanging out with immoral people.

This is where we enter young adulthood. We are somewhere on the spectrum of life from a well adjusted, reasonably mature, and secure person to an immature, troubled and insecure person. One end exhibits good and healthy choices in their daily life, such as personal discipline, moderation and responsibility. The other might demonstrate damaging and unhealthy decisions in their day-to-day activity, such as irresponsibility, drug use and extreme selfishness. All of us came through somewhere on this spectrum, I personally think I was on the more self-centered end.

It is probably obvious that if the teen makes it through adolescence on the healthy end of the spectrum, they are more likely to make good choices when the "big five" I listed in the first part of this chapter, come around. Conversely, someone who heads out of adolescence on the wilder end will be prone to continuing to make bad choices in facing their "big five."

It is now time to look at what I am calling the "big five" choices. We will start with "pairing off."

Pairing off

At its purest, this choice refers to the answer to the great relationship question, "Who am I going to spend the rest of my life with in marriage?"

In the cultures that value freedom and individuality, which are mostly what we know as western cultures, individuals typically make the choice of whom they will marry during young adulthood. Other cultures place some form of restriction on the individual and to varying degrees the family chooses marriage partners. We typically call these arranged marriages. Whether arranged or not, around the world it seems that most people get married in their late teens to early twenties.

There are also other pairing off relationships established at this time, such as living together with a view to marriage, living together for sexual convenience and homosexual pairings. Whatever kind of choice is made is largely determined by how a person handles the four SPAR questions (Security, Performance, Acceptance and Responsibility). As I dig into the forces that push us one direction or another on who we want to pair up with, I would like to start with what I would suggest is the best place to be, relationally speaking, a kind of base line. That is as someone who would normally be called a virgin in our society, but in my opinion is better described as a selfless individual. We will see why in a moment, but first I want to look at the marriage scripture(s).

Gen 2:18 - Then the Lord God said, "It is not good for the man to be alone; I will make him a helper suitable for him."

Gen 2:21-24 - So the Lord God caused a deep sleep to fall upon the man, and he slept; then He took one of his ribs and closed up the flesh at that place. The Lord God fashioned into a woman the rib which He had taken from the man, and brought her to the man. The man said, "This is now bone of my bones, and flesh of my flesh; She shall be called Woman, because she was taken out of Man." For this reason a man shall leave his father and his mother, and be joined to his wife; and they shall become one flesh.

These verses outline the reason I made the statement above about a selfless individual. Let us go through the thinking process together.

First, in verse 18 God said that it was not good for man to be alone, and He (God) would make a suitable helper for the man. God made the woman, meaning that only a woman is suitable for a man. This is in the context of a permanent relationship.

Next, in verse 23, the man identifies that the woman was taken out of him. This is both literal, meaning that God physically did this, and

116

psychological, meaning that the woman's Soul also came from the man. The man is declaring that he has a Soul connection, which we can also call deep intimacy, with the woman.

Lastly, in verse 24, it says that a man is to leave his parents and join in deep intimacy with a wife. This means that the man stays under the authority of his parents until he leaves to be with his wife. There is no in-between, no test relationships, no co-habitation, he is to be a physical and relational (in the context of deep intimacy) virgin as he goes into the marriage. (This, of course, strongly implies that this is true for a woman too.) Men are selfless because they have put their own natural desires on hold, while they wait for their "suitable helper." They have pre-committed to that unknown person who will fill the "suitable helper" part of their life.

This of course is the ideal situation. I know that since we are all imperfect we often fall short of this, but I have a point in going through this, and that is it gives us a baseline with which to compare all other courses of action in seeking a lifetime partner.

Having established a baseline, which is not my opinion, but is from the word of God, we can look at how our society looks compared to it. We are a miserable failure; let's look at why I can say that as a statement of truth. I'm simply going to make a short list:

1. We don't seem to be able to choose lifelong partners; the divorce rate in the US is 50% plus.
2. The level of sexually-transmitted diseases has been rising in our population for about 45 years.
3. Co-habitation is commonplace, whether for trial marriage or sexual convenience is irrelevant.
4. Homosexuality is on the increase, both male and female.

I hope it is acceptable to the reader to just make these broad statements, and to do it without citing sources. Having asked people I work with and socialize with, most people know these things to be accurate. In my discussions with others I made a truly amazing observation. These failures were all generally viewed as, normal and acceptable. We, as a group, seemed to have thrown out what always works, lifetime male to female marriages, and replaced them with inferior relationships. What is it about early adulthood that causes us to make inferior pairing decisions, and also inferior relational commitments?

The essence of the issue is very straightforward. What we believe about ourselves, in the deepest reaches of our Soul, determines how we will ultimately act in our pairing decisions. Let's overlay the SPAR methodology to analyzing our attempts at long-term pairing.

Starting with our personal sense of security (the "S" in SPAR), or how we feel about ourselves, we can see some things. If we believe that we are worthwhile, and have a strong belief in our ability to make wise decisions, we will tend to be reasonably secure. This will lead to us understanding our feelings toward other people, and in our context here, toward potential long-term partners. A more secure person is more likely to be able to make a good personal choice about who he or she wants to invest their time with and maybe ultimately pair off with. They are less likely to be overly influenced by others in their choice of a partner. The advantage of this is when making the actual or eventual choice of a permanent partner, the decision is owned, or emotionally bought into.

The less secure person is disadvantaged, and often highly disadvantaged, in being able to choose partners. Consider some of the things we identified as being present in the adolescent, from a personal security perspective. Emotional issues such as shame over who they are, fear of rejection and a sense of inadequacy are brought forward into young adulthood if they are unresolved. Coming right along with them are any coping behaviors the teen may have learned such as drinking too much alcohol, which of course maintains the propensity to fall into an emotional prison.

For the insecure person, meeting an individual who seems to fit with them may lead to premature decisions about sexual intimacy with an intent to make it permanent. As an example, a young man may use drinking as a way of temporarily dealing with insecurity, he may be what we call a party animal. Then he meets a young lady, who is also insecure, and lives life the same way. They have an immediate bond based on behavior, and begin a significant relationship. I'm guessing that we all know people who got married under these kinds of circumstances. The problem is that the relationship is not based on shared beliefs, values and attitudes, although they may have some of those. It is based on feeling better about oneself through destructive behaviors. Inevitably the relationship begins to deteriorate as one or both of the parties gets healthier, or gets worse in their compulsive activity. If they have married, separation is highly likely, and divorce is probable.

This kind of approach to looking at the pairing of insecure young adults can be made in any situation where acting out is occurring. Other examples could be shown using drug taking, sexual behavior, excelling in sports or overachieving at academics. The point is that pairing decisions of insecure people are made based on the wrong criteria or motivations, and are related more to behavioral patterns than shared values, beliefs and attitudes.

Let's move on to the "P" in SPAR; performance. It is probably easy to see how an individual who is performance oriented might be attracted to another person with the same orientation. For example two athletes could bond, based on their shared skills and passion for sports. When this bonding is based only on these things problems will often arise. What if one is a Buddhist and the other a Moslem? Or how about if one comes from a wealthy family and the other doesn't? Once the allure of sports diminishes or the ability to participate dwindles, the basis of relationship is gone. Again I ask; what if they are married? Trouble is highly possible.

The third factor of the SPAR method of analysis is "A" for acceptance, and for me this is the big one, the factor that causes the most problems in pairing.

As we found out in the previous chapter on adolescence, the lack of perceived acceptance is experienced as rejection, and a fear of rejection develops, if it is not already present in the Soul from childhood. The young adult living with this is constantly seeking to lessen or remove this fear from his or her Soul. This means, in the context of pairing, that they are going to gravitate toward people who seem to reduce this fear.

The prototype relationship here is, and I find this somewhat bizarre, where a people-pleaser provides acceptance for an individual needing it. This is where one person puts their emotional situation aside and links up with a person whose every choice in life revolves around themselves, to get acceptance. What a disaster! At some point the people-pleaser runs out of emotional input for the "acceptor" who basically sucks them emotionally dry, resulting in a relational breakdown. If they are married, it is big trouble, both sides experience frustration, pain, hurt and most likely anger. It has to be hard to recover from that.

There are even more damaging problems with a young adult struggling with acceptance in relationships. The most common is in the area of sexual behaviors. While I will be covering this subject in more detail later in the book, I would still like to discuss some of them here in the context of pairing in the young adult.

Assume that we have a young adult searching for acceptance in his or her life. It is reasonable to acknowledge that they will attach to somebody who pays them some attention, and recognize this as acceptance of them as a person. If the two of them bond together at some level, and it really doesn't have to be deep or intimate, the temptation to engage in sexual activity will arrive eventually. When both parties are agreeable, even if one or both has a value of not engaging in sexual activity until marriage, sex is likely to occur because the emotional desire for acceptance overrides the belief that pre-marital sex is wrong. Of course, if you don't have a strong belief about the right or wrong of sexual activity without appropriate commitment there is no barrier and sexual activity will happen faster.

Did you notice something here? I didn't identify the gender of either party, and this was deliberate. This simple behavioral scenario can be played out in heterosexual or homosexual situations. The heterosexual aspect is probably plain to all and can be thought of as a normal problem that has been around as long as humans have existed. The homosexual circumstance is more challenging to think through. For someone to allow himself or herself to engage in same gender sexual activity their beliefs about the natural order for sex have to be weak. This allows a person to have their desire for acceptance met through same sex relationships that have a physical component.

Once a person has engaged in sexual activity and found that they get their desire for acceptance fulfilled, the sexual activity can hook them. This means that if the relationship breaks down, as most do in this situation, the person with the high level of desire for acceptance is vulnerable to going though the whole process again. This leads to what we call promiscuity, and it can happen in both heterosexual and homosexual relationships.

Promiscuity inevitably leads to hurt as the relationships break up due to their unsound nature, that is that they are built on a driving desire for acceptance and sexual activity. The hurt is created in the Soul as things like betrayal through sexual unfaithfulness and abandonment are encountered. When enough hurt has accumulated inside the Soul, it can lead to severe emotional pain. Not only is the sexual activity an emotional trap, but the pain that goes with having your Heart broken so frequently may lead you into another emotional prison like drugs or drinking.

Some of this kind of behavioral trouble goes on during adolescence. Once the structure or boundaries of those years are lifted through things like moving out of the parent's home or earning a paycheck, the capability of engaging in promiscuity increases dramatically. This is why we see some young people who were restrained as teens seemingly go off the deep end in their relational choices when they hit college.

I've spent quite some time discussing acceptance and pairing behavior, because I think it is such a strong component of our behavioral choices in this area. My guess is that a lot of people reading this section of the book will identify with some of the things I've said. Some of us (like me as an example) will say something like this, "Aha, that is why I chose my first wife!"

Moving on now, let us look at how the SPAR factor of responsibility works in our pairing decisions. I want to remind the reader that this factor revolves around how we feel due to our ability to meet certain subjective standards. You may recall our discussion of being cool in the last chapter, which was the example we used to illustrate a subjective standard.

What can happen here is that as a young adult we often unconsciously adopt a subjective standard approach to picking our partners. We feel better about ourselves if we choose somebody who meets whatever standard is important to us. An example is that a good-looking young man we may look for an attractive young lady or how about one we can all understand, a young lady looks for someone who is like her dad.

I can't say that this method of choosing a partner is often going to be some kind of problem. At least it is based somewhat on values. The shortcoming of basing a choice of this kind on subjective standards is that as we mature we tend to change them or they may become less important, and sometimes we completely throw them out. If we have made a lifelong decision based on say, physical attractiveness, will that still be important to us when we are a few years older?

Now let me distill these four factors and their influence on our pairing choices down to a simple statement of a problem. If we base our choice of partner on how our feelings about ourselves lead us, this choice is very likely to become unsatisfactory later.

The primary result of this situation is, of course, a break-up. For a casual relationship this may not be difficult and for a serious committed relationship this can be very painful. However, for a marriage, divorce is most likely, it affects not just the pair involved, and is the most painful of all break-ups. I have been through a divorce, and for the very reasons I have been discussing; my relationship was not built on values, it was built on how I felt about myself. When I add up all the issues surrounding my first marriage I think the break-up was most likely one of the most painful experiences of my life, and it was self-inflicted.

The break-up of significant relationships takes its toll on a person. When we put ourselves into one and then it falls apart, we collect what is often called emotional baggage. Most people who read this have some baggage of their own, and can relate to the expression. The problem with baggage is this, we carry it around, and we bring it into new relationships, and share it. Emotional baggage is unresolved feelings, and we have a tendency to collect them. Examples of baggage that might be left after a break-up are; a sense of rejection, and feelings of failure, guilt and inadequacy.

Now let us take this discussion to the next step, a new relationship. We typically go into a new relationship with our baggage hidden in an emotional closet, knowing that if a new person saw it they may chose to not link up with us. Basically we lie. Eventually the baggage finds its way out of the closet, and gets shared. The chances are that both partners are bringing in baggage, sharing it with each other, making it a bigger problem. So now we have two flawed people trying to deal with their unresolved emotions in a new relationship, meaning that they can't actually focus on making the new relationship healthy.

You can probably see where I'm going here. When we partner as a young adult, if we do it based on how we feel about ourselves, we are most likely dooming ourselves to a series of relationships. Then as we have these relationships, emotional baggage accumulates, and character weaknesses begin to show and develop. Our response to the emotional baggage is most likely to be some form of compulsive behavior or even an addiction, such as using chemicals, sex, work or even religion. Emotional prisons all of them! No matter whether we stay unpaired or end up in a totally monogamous relationship, or even marriage, these prisons will still exist.

If you or anybody you know is considering entering into a significant relationship, whether it is new or a current one that is going deeper, God has some great advice.

2 Cor 6:14 - Do not be bound together with unbelievers; for what partnership have righteousness and lawlessness, or what fellowship has light with darkness?

It specifically instructs Christians to not get bound, get partnered, or get paired up with non-Christians. In the verses that follow this instruction it is explained a little more, and a principle is established; that is, only team up with people who have similar values, beliefs and attitudes. I hope you recognize these as the characteristics of the Heart, which we have discussed throughout the book. This principle is valid whether you believe as a Christian or not. For example, two atheists are more likely to have a successful, mutually satisfying and long lasting, relationship than an atheist and a Moslem.

Finally, we can say this. Young adulthood brings many moments of significant personal choice into our lives, and none of these is of greater importance than who we partner with in our deeper and intimate relationships. There is an old saying that goes something like this, "Behind every great man is a great woman." While we can debate this, it does illustrate the truth that our choices on partners are a major determining factor of the outcomes, like achievements, in our lives.

Further Education

Another important choice we make is whether we want to study after adolescence, and what we are going to get further educated about. For most of us, we enter into decisions about what we are going to do after high school, before we actually leave, and while we are in our late teen years. It seems almost routine to us as we move through high school years. We either are or are not going to college, and we are going to study what we like or think we will like.

Most of us, however, have not really thought things through. Many, many mistakes are made in this part of our lives with respect to our academics. In my own life I can see this played out. I was told I wasn't good enough to go to university. Looking back, I think that was a horrific statement from the headmaster (principal) at my high school. So I chose at 18 to go into the workforce, got a job where I would be paid to work and go to school part-time. Four years later, I had an honors degree in Physics and Chemistry from the University of London. So not only was the high school wrong about my academic capabilities, but I actually excelled, ending up as a top student. The big problem was, I really wasn't that interested in science as a career!

What had happened was I had made a choice based on factors that were external to my Soul, when the choice of what to do in life ought to be based on internal factors. The school system in England where I grew up was responding to the problem of not having enough scientists and engineers to fill the demand of industry. So I was channeled down the road of science, and I didn't have a clue! Because I didn't score well in some science tests, I was thought of as not being good enough to go to college. My natural abilities took over, allowing me to succeed and exceed the expectations of those around me. I did well, but it was still a sub-optimal choice, because inside my Soul, I wasn't interested in science.

Have you ever thought about the decisions on schooling as Soul decisions? Probably not, but they are! They have far-reaching and sometimes eternal consequences. In my own case, if I hadn't chosen to get a job in a science-oriented field, I would not have gone to work in Saudi Arabia (as a scientist). Then I wouldn't have been moved into management by that company, I wouldn't have changed careers and worked and obtained an MBA from a US university, and I most likely would not have come to the United States. The eternal consequence may have been that I wouldn't have been in an environment where I would have gone to a church and become a Christian.

While the final outcome of my original choice, and all the subsequent choices, may have worked out, it took about 30 years to get where I am today. That infers, quite rightly, that there was a lot of wasted time and effort in my life, looking at it from a human viewpoint. (My personal view is that it took a long time for God to mold my flawed character into what it is today, mostly due to my stubbornness.) I see this kind of story played out so often in the lives of people I know. The problem is that wrong choices in personal academic decisions can steer us into the direction of an emotional prison later in life.

Now let us look at this decision area of "Further Education" in terms of the SPAR method of analysis. We'll begin with "Security." You may recall that here we are looking at the question, "How do I feel about myself." I don't think that the answer to that question will impact the choice of where to go, and what to study, the other three SPAR factors will be more relevant. The exception might be on the issue of if we are going to go to college or not.

I can see that if we are insecure, meaning not feeling positive about ourselves, we might want to avoid college, and all the stress it will bring. We probably all know individuals who have elected to do something other than higher education in their early adulthood, even though they are fully academically qualified to get in a school. I'm not talking about the person who can't get in for family, social or financial reasons. I'm talking about the people who are allowing fear, due to a lack of feeling good about themselves, to stop them. In the end, they are likely to regret this as they consign themselves to a work role that doesn't suit their abilities. This in itself can lead to further erosion of self-image, and nudge them toward taking up an activity that leads them toward an emotional prison later. I have met a couple of men who chose to not go to college and study mechanical engineering. They elected instead to become auto mechanics, which is a worthy profession, but regretted it because they knew they could have gone further. Both ended up as alcoholics. The good news is that they have both quit drinking, and have reached an acceptance of their choices and the outcomes.

The second SPAR factor is "Performance." "How do I feel about myself, due to the things I do?" For the young adult, there is a lot of feedback in the context of further education. Test scores, grades, acceptance letters and scholarships received all provide data into the Soul through the gateway of the Will. The young adult will contemplate these things, and may even seek counsel in an effort to figure out where he or she should go, and what to study.

The choice is going to be driven toward a school and an academic subject that, in the opinion of the individual, will lead to more good feelings about personal performance. For example, a person who has an affinity for animals may choose to go to a college with a school for veterinarians, because they have always felt good about themselves and the way they handled animals.

If a young adult doesn't go with a choice that fits in with how they feel due to their behaviors, they will almost inevitably begin to think and feel about themselves negatively. Using our vet example, if the individual goes into a medical track school, intending to become a doctor, they might experience high levels of dissatisfaction in their studies, as they no longer interact with animals. It is entirely possible that a young adult will not be in touch with what they are experiencing, and choose to act out or get into some form of coping behavior. And, as has been said before, this can easily lead to other things, and into an emotional prison.

The third SPAR factor, "Acceptance," is the most important, in choices about higher education. Two things are always present in our choice of college or other further education. Where do I go and what do I study? While these seem like straightforward questions, they may have several alternative answers. The problems begin when we answer them from sub-optimal reasoning. By this I mean reasoning having a high degree of emotions attached to them. Let us look at some of the variables here.

Maybe, when we are looking at where to go we only look at where our parents have been, or where our siblings went or where a significant person in our lives is going. It is easy to see that choosing on the basis of relationships can mean that we head off to a school that doesn't really match our capabilities or needs. We feel that we should go where mom or dad went, or maybe we want to avoid mom or dad feeling rejected because we didn't choose her or his school. Perhaps we feel that we would like to go to the same school as our high school sweetheart. We might even want to go where, all our friends, are going.

Or maybe we choose a study subject like engineering, because our father and brother are both engineers. Or possibly we go to get a degree in education, because our grandfather and mother were both teachers. We might even consider communications as a subject because a couple of the popular kids at high school are doing that. Another kind of choice could be that we are going to the same school as our high school sweetheart, but we have to pick a discipline that is acceptable, but not what we really want.

These alternatives are all due to the answer to the question, "How do I feel about myself due to my perception of what others feel and think about me?" If other people's opinions are highly important to us, we will choose a school and subject based on what we believe they think and feel about us and our activities. How many people have gone to their parent's alma mater to please one or more of them?

When we base this decision on our own perception of others thoughts and feelings we are trapped from the very beginning. Wherever we are studying and whatever we are learning, will not help, we are doomed to end up feeling resentments. We may even blame others for being forced to study chemistry, when we really wanted to learn about sociology. Maybe we also didn't really want to go to a big school and would have preferred a smaller campus.

The problem with resentments is that they are like emotional cancers; they start small and grow, and eventually take over our Soul. As a young adult, sometimes the only way we know how to deal with them is to act out. So we start to party, or drop out, or do something equally self-destructive. Many of our responses to resentments involve behaviors that eventually trap us in emotional prisons.

The last SPAR factor is "Responsibility." And here we answer the question, "How do I feel about myself, due to my ability to meet specific standards?" I wonder how many kids have applied and gone to a school because it was the place to be? I live in Texas, and of course the University of Texas is the place so many people want to go to. You will certainly get a fine education there, assuming you complete your studies. However, it has so much more going on, a great athletic program, a wonderful environment and a lively social scene. The young adult may consider Texas as the place to be, not because he or she can get a fine education, but because they can feel good about the social scene.

Problems begin when the social part of life inevitably interferes with academic performance. Low grades may be one result, but worse than that, a student may be forced to drop out. Then we have new issues, like failure, bitterness and resentments, beginning to appear. These things can lead to coping behaviors like self-medication with prescription drugs. And, as I have said many times, these eventually lead to emotional prisons.

I think I've said enough about the subject of a young adult's choices around higher education, and we can now move on to a closely related subject, choice of career.

Career

I think this significant choice that is made by a young adult is closely allied to further education which we have just discussed. Although a career is not cast in concrete when we choose a school and academic course, we usually have something in mind about what we want to do in life. For example, if we study music at a music school like Juilliard, we are probably thinking about becoming a professional musician, but if we choose music and study at a seminary, we are contemplating becoming a worship minister of some kind.

Many of the same kinds of arguments and reasoning that we used when discussing our choices in higher education can be used when we look at the big decision of what career path to pursue. For this reason I am not going to go through a detailed look at how each of the SPAR factors affects career choice. Rather than that I am going to look at some of the more important effects these factors have on career choice.

Starting with a sense of insecurity, whether derived from simply not feeling self-confident or from the SPAR acceptance or performance factors, we can easily imagine what might happen. A young adult could be faced with a possibility of no job offers coming out of high school or college. They could also be on the other end, having several offers. The problem arises when a choice has to eventually be made. Lacking self-confidence can often result in taking the first thing offered, or going through the agony of trying to choose which offer is best, and worrying that you might be making the wrong choice.

Most of us older folks know and understand that it is not a lifetime living death sentence to take the wrong job at eighteen or twenty two years of age. The young insecure adult doesn't have the benefit of a few gray hairs though. Let's take a trip into their Soul and try to see what might be happening, remembering that there could be a myriad of variations on how a young adult deals with this issue.

The young adult who is feeling insecure is facing this type of situation. They know they need to take a job, they understand that their time has come to fully contribute, economically speaking, to their own upkeep. They are searching through their life's experiences seeking the internal wisdom to help them with this decision. I'm sure you noticed that these are all characteristics of the Mind. In the Heart, I picture the young adult as pedaling furiously in low gear, going round and round, but not getting very far. This is because our young adult is lacking in self-confidence, and is having a hard time figuring out which beliefs, values and attitudes apply in this job or career choice. The Will is operating with its gateway wide open as the young man or woman is seeking input on the choice to be made.

In this scenario, we can see how easy it could be for a young adult to get off track behaviorally and to make an unwise choice. There is internal pressure in the Soul, resulting in emotions that may be difficult to deal with, such as distress or anxiety. If the young adult is used to acting out, that is what they will turn to in order to relieve themselves. So for example, if they are drug-takers, that is where they head, the pill bottle or needle. The choice of what to do is then likely to be made while they are in a period of acting out in their lives. I'm sure you would agree that it is highly probable they will make a less than optimal decision. I can also see that they may even choose not to choose, and reject every opportunity, as they are controlled by their emotional state. Not choosing anything, is of course because they are in an emotional prison, which in my example is a chemical prison.

The most common outcome is the choice that directs the young adult into a career that doesn't fit with their abilities, desires and training. For example, a person may choose to go into the military after getting a degree in architectural engineering, because their dad did, but they really wanted to design big buildings. In this example, acceptance within the family is a big problem. It might be sourced from the father who pushes his child, or it might be the child trying to please his or her parents.

I could detail many examples, as I'm sure you could, of this type of less than optimal decision-making. The real problem though is that less than satisfactory career choices can lead to negative emotions within the individual, and if unresolved, this points a person toward coping behaviors and ultimately, emotional prison.

Location

Where do I want to live? This is another big choice for a young adult. For some people at eighteen, the answer is simple; anywhere but in my parent's home! For others it is something like, "I'm staying at my parent's place, I won't have any expenses." The person going off to college is making a deferred choice as they work through their years of higher education, but still faces it on completion.

What is the big deal about where I live? I have actually heard this many times, and I find it an incredible question. This is as big an issue as what school do I go to, or what career am I going into. Where we live will determine what values, beliefs and attitudes we are exposed to. Most likely, we will take on some of these things as our own. If we look at this from the perspective of how our Soul operates we can see why. As we live in a new place (or social environment); we encounter new beliefs, values and attitudes. Our Will lets these in through its gateway and our Heart encounters something new and different. A young adult with strongly held views might constantly push these new alternatives aside; a person with a limited or loose moral mooring might not, and allow these new alternative views to change him or her. I do want to say here that moral mooring doesn't imply right or wrong, it just refers to the fact that we all have one. A few examples might help.

I want to start with a personal example. I grew up in England, and was exposed to the view that "Britannia rules the waves" or some variation of it. This is one way of saying that people in the UK think their way is best, and that was part of my belief system. Then I moved to Saudi Arabia, which struck me as a step down culturally, which I'm sure a Saudi person wouldn't agree with, and reinforced my belief on which was best. However, I worked with Americans, who thought their way was best. This was all very eye opening of course. I came to appreciate that no one has the corner on what is best, and there are good and not so good points about all societies. My point here is that I came to believe (new beliefs replaced old ones) that I would be in a better place, internally, that is from a Soul perspective, if I lived and worked in America. A location decision! My family in the UK probably think I'm some kind of traitor, which is not true, I still love my country of birth, and all my family over there. I now see that when you live in the UK you don't get a true picture of what America is all about. This confirms that where you live can influence a lot of your values.

But let's look at just inside the US. If you move to San Francisco, you will be exposed to very pro-homosexual values, beliefs and attitudes. If you move to Atlanta, it will be heavily pro-African-American values, beliefs and attitudes. If you live in Salt Lake City, it will be pro-family and pro-Mormon. Wyoming and Montana will be pro-gun. It is easy to see that this is true; every part of the country has its own characteristics. The important point here is that wherever we live will influence our Heart. This influence may or may not change what we believe in, but it is still there.

At its core, what I have called a location decision for the young adult is really a "people I associate with" choice. Places don't actually have values, beliefs and attitudes; it is the people who live there who usually determine by consensus what the local values are. This is not always true as we see that in some places a minority group determining what the values, beliefs and attitudes are. Nevertheless, we can all be influenced by the values, beliefs and attitudes that exist in the place we choose to live.

This reminds me of another of my favorite verses from Scripture, it is found in 1st Corinthians 15:33, which says:

Do not be deceived: "Bad company corrupts good morals."

Pretty clear isn't it? Who you hang out with influences you.

Let's take a moment or two to look at what happens when we move to another place as young adults, and how it can contribute to putting us onto a path toward an emotional prison. First, we can acknowledge that we begin by being in a familiar place, which we normally call home. We are in a place, among a group of people we know, normally family, that provides us with some form of consistency in our lives. Our values, beliefs and attitudes have been formed in this environment, and we, for the most part, have a comfort with this situation. What we may not connect with very well, is that this environment protects us, not in the physical sense, but in the sense of our Soul. We have an umbrella of protection over us. So that when we are assaulted with unfamiliar values, we can rely on the people we associate with to help us deal with them, and usually reject them.

Moving away from home, but still living nearby in the physical sense enables us to keep some of the umbrella of protection in place. This is also somewhat true when, as young adults, we move to a college that is reasonably close to where our family is, as we have reasonably frequent contact with our family of origin. In both these situations the umbrella continues to do its work of protection. When we move a large distance away, what I have called the location effect begins to operate.

A general example of this in the US would be when a young person moves to a college in another state. If they come from a conservative background, they will probably encounter a large number of alternative values, beliefs and attitudes, and will be unprotected by their family. Let us say that they are individuals who, using the SPAR method of analysis, are subject to internal or Soul difficulties due to negative feelings about themselves when experiencing non-acceptance (A) or responsibility (R). It is easy to see that they may succumb to the temptation to change their values, beliefs and attitudes to fit in.

The same point can be made about any young person who moves away from the family to another place, for any reason. They are going to find themselves subject to this temptation to change the values, beliefs and

131

attitudes that reside in their Heart. What can also happen is that a person who moves location can end up with two or more conflicting values, beliefs or attitudes. This is where the root of some emotional prisons can be found.

Let's say that a young person grows up with a value, a belief or an attitude that spending time with family during the holidays is important. Then when he or she moves away, they find themselves in a group that has a value, a belief or an attitude that spending time with the group is important. It is possible that they will take on the new value, belief or attitude, without releasing the old one. This means that both exist in their Heart, and they conflict. It is easy to see that a feeling of guilt may arise inside the Soul, when the holiday season rolls around, and they choose family over group, or vice-versa. The question of how this guilt is dealt with is interesting. Most of us might accept it, and live with it. Some of us, however, struggle with the conflict and the guilt. This can lead us to try to resolve the negative feelings using a joint of marijuana or a fifth of Scotch, both entryways to an emotional prison.

There are many, many ways we encounter emotional troubles when we change locations. For the most part, they get resolved, but sometimes they don't. The young adult moving permanently away from where he or she was raised is at risk of having to give up some of their long held, and sometimes cherished, values, beliefs and attitudes. This can create problems inside the Soul, which can then lead to us developing coping mechanisms, which in the extreme, point us to an emotional prison.

Social Group

This is the last of the big five choices we make as a young adult, and it is really a derivative of the other four. I have talked about whom you associate with as being an important contributing factor in getting into, or keeping out of, an emotional prison. In the last section I mentioned a Bible verse (1 Cor 15:33) that said something like this. "Who you hang out with, affects your values, beliefs and attitudes."

While that last paraphrase is always true in every phase of our lives, it is most important during the young adult stage of life. Let me explain why. It is here that we come out from the family environment and as I said before, any protection it offers. Prior to this, we have family who can help us see the character of the people we are around, and help us to choose our friends. Also, prior to being a young adult we are in social groups who, generally speaking, have similar values, attitudes and beliefs to our own. These things change as we get into young adulthood.

Think about all the new social encounters we have as we move on in life. We meet new people at college, at the new job, and at the new locations we live in. All of these have the potential to influence our values, beliefs and attitudes dramatically. The closer we allow some of these new social acquaintances to come to us, the more they are likely to affect our Heart as we open the gateway of our Will to their input. The person we choose to pair up with will be the person that is likely to influence us the most. In fact, we could even define closeness in this way. Closeness is the degree to which we open the gateway of our Soul to another person.

These new social encounters provide new friends with different values, beliefs and attitudes. We start going to new social events, we attend new churches, we go to different bars and clubs, we join new organizations, we take up new activities and we often turn our world upside down because of this new social life. Every person we meet has the potential to affect or influence our values, beliefs and attitudes.

When I was eighteen, I began attending a college near where I lived and began pursuing my bachelors degree. I didn't know it beforehand but it was a hotbed of communist activity in England. One of the lecturers was a bigwig in the local trade union organizations and a leading member of the communist party. His role at the college was to meet the young students, like me, and persuade them to join the cause. It provided some interesting discussion times in the college bar! For the record, I never took him up on his offers of significance like "you'll be doing some great things for the people" or "we need to bring down the government." I didn't join the party, and I have never been affiliated with any political parties, although I have strong opinions.

It is a great example of what can happen in young adulthood. In this case there was a proactive effort by more mature, or at least older, adults to influence for a purpose. Whether it is purposed or non-purposed, the outcome is still the same. Our Heart's values, beliefs and attitudes are under attack, or they are at least under self-review.

The practical effects of this in our lives seem to me to fall in two main categories. The first would be that we would continue to pick people to be close to with a discerning approach. We would seek only those that have similar values, beliefs and attitudes. This would be the safest course of action, in the sense that we would be able to retain our internal moral compass without exposing it to too many outside or alternative ideas. It is likely that our life will be similar in young adulthood to what it was in adolescence. If we have certain proclivities in our youth we would continue them. For example, if we dealt with negative emotions with alcohol, we would continue to drink to appease them. If we were, however, a person of moderation, and had learned to handle life's difficulties as they come along, we would carry right along in that mode.

The second broad practical effect is that of change, change of the Heart, of one's values, beliefs and attitudes. Consider the person who is driven by how they feel about themselves. We can think in terms of the SPAR approach and see that if this person is insecure, or maybe needs acceptance or simply wants to fit in to a newly established social group, then they are vulnerable to being influenced. By this, I mean that are much more likely to open up the gateway of their Will, and allow new values, beliefs and attitudes to come into their Soul. Some of these will stay in the Heart and replace or sit alongside old values, beliefs and attitudes. This is what we know as a changed Heart.

Normally we like to think of a changed Heart as a positive change, but there is nothing sacrosanct about that; the change could also be detrimental or negative. If we are motivated by a desire to fit in we may alter our values, beliefs and attitudes to accommodate our secret wants. We have all heard about freshmen college students who go off the deep end. All that is happening is that they are being influenced by others to change their internal values, beliefs and attitudes and when you add in the opportunity to act out, off they go. That is why the most effective way of dealing with that kind of situation is to bring them home, which gets them away from the influences and away from the opportunities.

Hopefully we can all see how easy it is to slip into new behaviors as we see a change in our social circle as a result of moving into young adulthood. If these behaviors are coping mechanisms, or a way of medicating our negative feelings about ourselves then we may slip right into some form of emotional prison like drugs or sexual addiction.

A Word About Later Adulthood

I don't intend to cover in any specific way the period after young adulthood. I am doing this for two reasons. The first is that the SPAR analytical method could be applied to later adulthood, but it wouldn't be a much different discussion than we have already had. The second is that I will be covering the actual emotional prisons from the perspective of later adulthood anyway.

Following this chapter there is a short one summarizing everything in the first ten chapters. I'm doing this to refresh us all on what we have learned, and get us ready to see how it all comes together in real life for those in emotional prisons.

11

SO FAR, SO GOOD!

To look backward for a while is to refresh the eye, to restore it, and to render it the more fit for its prime function of looking forward.
Margaret Fairless Barber

We have now come to the end of this first of three books. This is where we are going to transition from being somewhat theoretical to being more practical, from looking at our subject of emotional prisons clinically to seeing how acting out is played out in our lives. After this short chapter, book two Emotional Prisons – Prisons will begin a series of chapters detailing out actual examples of emotional prisons, and then the third and last book Emotional Prisons – Healing will address the matter of getting out of prison, which I prefer to call healing.

Starting Point

At the beginning of the book we identified what an emotional prison is, we defined it this way:

An emotional prison is a place where a person's life is controlled by his or her feelings.

We learned that a good way of thinking about how any of us end up in an emotional prison is that it is the place we go as a result of acting out. Acting out is short for acting out of our emotions, and we stated that this is something that we have all done, but for some of us it is a way of dealing with life, with the result being we get trapped.

At this point we took a look at two general spiritual aspects of the subject. We looked at the overall subject as a battle, a spiritual battle, between God and His arch foe, Satan, over the Souls of men. We identified that it is one of Satan's tactics to try to influence a person into getting him or herself into an emotional prison. To illustrate the reason why Satan would do this we categorized people as believers or non-believers in God. For non-believers, Satan is attempting to keep us away from God, for believers he is trying to make our lives miserable and spiritually ineffective. Believing in God does not exempt a person from finding himself or herself trapped!

136

The second general spiritual aspect of this whole subject is what exactly gets trapped. It was stated that the battle is over the Souls of men, and so we identified what a Soul is, and why it is important. We showed that our Soul was the part of us that is made in the image of God, and just like God, it is physically invisible to us, but nevertheless exists.

Three Chapters

The next three chapters were spent explaining what the Soul is. We described how it is made up of three intimately linked parts, the Mind, the Heart and the Will. We then identified how these three parts had three characteristics each and we specified them. Here is a simple summary:

1. Mind – Knowledge, Understanding and Wisdom
2. Heart – Values, Beliefs and Attitudes
3. Will – Choice, Control and Gateway

In those three chapters we showed how these nine characteristics are interdependent, not being able to function fully on their own. Examples of how these work together are found throughout the series of books, and we will be seeing more when we talk about actual prisons.

Early Childhood

Chapters 5, 6 and 7 covered looking at the some of the things that happen to us as children that lay the groundwork for us to get pointed at an emotional prison later in life. We looked at the period from conception to early adolescence and focused on two major events that tend to steer our whole lives, if they happen to us. They are abandonment and abuse.

With abandonment we identified that while some abandonment is only physical, which is easy to identify, all abandonment is psychological, meaning of the Soul. We can be abandoned while living in the home of our family of origin; we can actually feel alone when there is a whole family around us.

When we discussed abuse, we looked at both the abuser and the victim, to see what was actually happening inside their Souls. We saw that abuse involves the pushing of one person's choices out of the gateway of their own Will through the gateway of another person's Will. When a child is the victim we call that child abuse, and it comes in several types as described in Chapter 7. Abuse is also always psychological, and is sometimes physical as well.

SPAR

We introduced a method, in Chapter 8, of looking at, or analyzing, people's behavioral characteristics called SPAR. This helps us to understand how an individual gets trapped by their acting out, often ending up in an emotional prison. SPAR factors begin to exert themselves in adolescence and continue to work throughout our lives.

Let us go over what SPAR actually is:

1. Security – Looks at how secure we feel about ourselves.
2. Performance – Addresses the question, "How do I feel about myself, due to what I do?"
3. Acceptance – This is about answering the question, "How do others feel about me?"
4. Responsibility – Is a recognition that we all have an internal personal accountability, and that we face the challenge, 'How do I feel about myself, due to my ability to meet specific standards?"

It is these four factors that are primarily responsible for us falling into an emotional prison. There is typically one dominant factor, but some of us may have more than one operating in our lives.

Adolescence

In Chapter 9 we looked at the period of time known as adolescence. We identified that this period is significant in many cultures around the world and generally begins around 13 years of age and finishes at about 19 years old. It was postulated that when a child moves into adolescence they enter into Self phase of their lives. I described it as a Self switch being turned on, where the teen suddenly realizes that they have control over their own Soul, and that means everything is about them. One of the big problems, however, is that they don't have fully developed Soul skills such as reasoning, emotional control or moderation.

We looked at six characteristics commonly found in the lives of adolescents and analyzed them using the SPAR method. We saw how by using the SPAR approach we can demonstrate that they way an adolescent answers the SPAR questions in their life's actions could point them into the direction of an emotional prison. These six characteristics are:

1. Disillusionment, disenchantment or disappointment.
2. Becoming increasingly dishonest and deceptive.
3. Denial of actual emotions, and substitution of others.
4. Avoiding responsibility and commitment.
5. Become more self-centered, self-conscious and self-reliant.
6. Increasingly influenced by others.

Of particular importance for a teen is the SPAR factor of acceptance, where we saw how rejection or fear of rejection can play a prominent part in their decision-making with respect to getting involved in self-medicating activities such as sex or drugs. And of course these kinds of responses can lead into the longer-term problems of emotional prisons.

Early Adulthood

The chapter immediately preceding this one was about the period I called "early adulthood", which I defined as from about 18 to 25 years of age. Here we saw that life starts to become more complex as we leave the nest or the protection of our family of origin. We noted that there were five major decisions that we generally make in early adulthood. These were:

1. Pairing off
2. Further Education
3. Career
4. Location
5. Social group

We looked at these five areas of choices in the context of our SPAR method of analyzing Soul behavior. We discovered that any one of these choices could increase our likelihood of developing an acting out response and thereby pointing us toward an emotional prison. We learned that as a general rule the people we associated with in early adulthood have a significant influence over us. This influence can be so strong that our response will often be to change values, beliefs and attitudes we have held our entire lives. This kind of internal change could then lead to new behaviors, some of which may not be to our benefit, and will lead us on the path to an emotional prison.

What Next?

There are two parts to the book series left. The next book covers the actual prisons that I have alluded to throughout the book, and the third and last book covers the subject of getting out of prison, or healing as I prefer to call it.

The prisons I am going to cover in the next book are:

Religion, False Intimacy, Additives, Victimhood, People Pleasing, Perfectionism, Risk-Taking, and Other Prisons.

In the last book I cover healing in three parts.

Ten Principles of Healing.
Twelve Barriers to Healing.
Seven Healing Choices.

Appendix A

Books and Other Resources mentioned in Emotional Prisons.

In Book 2 – Emotional Prisons - Prisons

Chapter 13.

The Quran, University of Michigan translation.

The River War – Sir Winston Churchill. (1899 version)

The Arab Mind – Raphael Patai

Chapter 14.

The Jesus Seminar, an organization.

Christianity In Crisis – Hank Hanegraaff, chapter on dysfunctional Christianity.

Love and Respect – Emerson Eggerichs.

Chapter 15.

Addicted to Love – Stephen Arterburn. (Not referenced, but still a good book to read on the issue of false intimacy.)

God's Grace and the Homosexual Next Door – Alan Chambers.

Intimacy needs resources:

1. Parenting with Intimacy (Workbook suggested) by Dr. David and Teresa Ferguson, Dr. Paul and Vicky Warren and Terri Ferguson.
2. Discovering Intimacy Workbook, by Ferguson and Walker.
3. Go to www.greatcommandment.net for a more complete listing.

The Search for Significance – Robert McGee

Chapter 16.

Yale study mentioned is reported in Journal of Pediatrics, Feb 1996 by William Tamborlane M.D. et al. of Yale University.

Chapter 18.

Co-dependent no more – Melody Beattie.

Co-Dependence – Healing the Human Condition by Charles L. Whitfield.

http://www.codependents.org/ The CODA worldwide website.

Chapter 20.

Mere Christianity – C. S. Lewis

Chapter 21.

Dress For Success – John Molloy

http://sites.google.com/site/clutterersanonymous/Home The website for people dealing with clutter that offers a 12 step solution.

In Book 3 – Emotional Prisons - Healing

Chapter 26.

Shame – The Exposed Self – Michael Lewis

Chapter 28.

Safe People – Henry Cloud and John Townsend.

Celebrate Recovery – www.celebraterecovery.com

Al-Anon - www.al-anon.alateen.org

Appendix B

Scripture References used by Chapter

In Book 1 – Emotional Prisons - Origins

Chapter 1. - 2 Pet 2:9, Gen 1:26-27, Jn 4:24, Mk 12:30, Mt 28:19.

Chapter 2. - Isa 55:8-9, 2 Tim 3:16-17, Jas 1:17, Mt 23:23, 1 Sam 15:29, Pr 1:7, Pr 9:10, 1 Kings 4:29.

Chapter 3. - Mt 22:36-40, Ps 119:105, Rom 10:9-10, Jn 14:6, Jer 12:3, Ecc 11:9, Jer 17:9.

Chapter 4. - Gen 2:16-17, 1 Cor 7:5, 2 Pet 1:5-8, Gal 5:23-23, Mt 11:27 (Lk 10:22), Jn 14:6.

Chapter 5. - Mal 2:16, Dt 31:6.

Chapter 6. - Pr 4:23, Jer 17:9, Col 3:21.

Chapter 7. - Eph 5:11-13, Lk 17:1-2, Ex 20:14.

Chapter 8. - Ex 20:3-17.

Chapter 9. - Jas 1:8, Rom 15:7, Pr 22:6.

Chapter 10. - Mt 7:24-27, Gen 2:21-24, Gen 2:18, 2 Cor 6:14, 1 Cor 15:33.

In Book 2 – Emotional Prisons - Prisons

Chapter 12. - Dt 18:9-12.

Chapter 13. - Dt 7:6, Gen 12:2-3, Jn 11:47-53.

Chapter 14. - Rom 3:23, Heb 11:1, Eph 2:8-9, Mt 28:18-20, Eph 5:33, Eph 6:12, Ps 8:4.

Chapter 15. - Jn 10:30, Jn 17:20-23, Lev 18:22, Pr 6:16-19, Job 31:1-3.

Chapter 16. - 3 Jn 2, 1 Cor 6:19-20.

143

Chapter 17. - Gen 4:13-14, Gen 4:6-7, Pr 29:18.

Chapter 18. - Rev Ch 6, Jdg Ch 14-16, Gal 1:10.

Chapter 19. - Col 3:23.

Chapter 20. - Mt 25:14-28, Mt 16:26.

Chapter 21. - Lk 16:13, Mt 12:26, 1 Cor 14:40, Ps 96:1-2.

Chapter 22. - Gen 2:25, Jer 31:13.

In Book 3 – Emotional Prisons - Healing

Chapter 23. - Ex 15:26(d), Ps 41:4, Ps 103:3, Ps 107:19-20, Ps 147:3, Isa 53:4-5, 2 Ki 5:1-14, 2 Cor 12:7-9, Jn 5:5-6, Jas 5:13-16, 1 Cor 12:28.

Chapter 24. - 1 Ki 11:4, Ecc 12:13-14, Mt 11:28-30, Jer 6:16, Jn 16:33, Mt 7:24-27, Pr 14:27, Pr 16:25, Mt 4:4, 2 Chr 7:14, Rom 10:9, Lk 5:25-26.

Chapter 25. - 1 Jn 1:6, Jn 12:37-40, Isa 6:9-10, Pr 16:18, Dan 4:37, Ps 86:5, Mt 6:12, Mt 6:14-15, Ps 32:3-5, Ps 69:29.

Chapter 26. - Gen 2:25, Gen 3:7-10, Ex 20:2, Ex 20:3, Isa 58:11, Jer 31:25, Eph 6:12, Eph 6:13, Ecc 4:9-10, Isa 43:18-19, Isa 5:13-14, Pr 1:29-33, Eph 4:30-32, Mt 6:15.

Chapter 27. - Lk 5:17, Pr 9:10, Isa 11:2-3, Acts 9:31, Pr 10:27, Pr 14:26, Pr 14:27, Pr 16:6, Pr 19:23, Pr 22:4, Pr 2:1-5, Ps 119:11, 1 Cor 2:14, Lev 26:3(a), Lev 26:11-12, Phil 2:8, Josh 24:14-15, Jer 17:9, Pr 4:23, Lam 3:40, Jn 8:31-32.

Chapter 28. - Ps 32:5, Jas 5:16, 1 Jn 1:9, Gal 6:2, 2 Cor 5:16, 2 Cor 7:10, Pr 11:14, 1 Cor 15:33, Pr 13:20, Isa 32:6, Pr 17:12, Mt 22:39.

Chapter 29. - 2 Cor 10:5, Pr 22:7, Jn 8:44, 2 Cor 10:5 (Msg), Heb 4:12, 1 Cor 10:13, Eph 5:33, Jas 4:3, Ps 77:5-6, Phil 2:12-13, Eph 4:22-24, 1 Cor 15:31 (Amp), Rom 12:2, Lam 3:40.

Chapter 30. - Rom 3:23, Isa 53:6, Jas 4:1-2, 2 Tim 3:16-17.

www.ingramcontent.com/pod-product-compliance
Lightning Source LLC
Chambersburg PA
CBHW070347300526

45791CB00023B/425